Working for Yourself in the
ARTS·&·CRAFTS

Second Edition

Sarah Hosking

**KOGAN
PAGE**

Dedicated to colleagues and friends at East Midlands Arts 1972–81, since leaving whose companionship for self-employment I have learnt most of the lessons here described.

First published in Great Britain in 1986 by
Kogan Page Limited, 120 Pentonville Road,
London N1 9JN.
Second edition 1989

British Library Cataloguing in Publication Data
Hosking, Sarah
   Working for yourself in the arts and
   crafts.—2nd ed.
   1. Great Britain. Artists and craftsmen.
   Self-employment. Manuals
   I. Title
   658′.041

   ISBN 1-85091-717-5

Typeset by DP Photosetting, Aylesbury, Bucks
Printed and bound in Great Britain by
Biddles Limited, Guildford

Acknowledgements

I should like to record my thanks to several colleagues and friends who have advised on the compilation of this manuscript and to the staff of the Arts Council Art Department, the Crafts Council and to Millicent Bowerman of the Gulbenkian Foundation. In particular my thanks are due to Margot Coatts, freelance exhibition organiser and writer, Adrian Barr-Smith, a solicitor with Denton, Hall, Burgin and Warren and formerly Director of Artlaw, and Peter Jones, Director of the Welsh Arts Council Art Department, all of whom have contributed generously their time and attention.

March 1986 Sarah Hosking

'When I was at school, on certain afternoons we all had to do what was called Labour – weeding, sweeping, sawing logs for the boiler room, that kind of thing; but if you had a chit from Matron you were let off to spend the afternoon messing about in the Art Room. Labour or Art. And you've got a chit for *Life? (passionately) Where did you get it?* What is an artist? For every thousand people there's nine hundred doing the work, ninety doing well, nine doing good, and one lucky bastard who's the artist.'

Tom Stoppard *Travesties* 1975 (Faber & Faber)

Contents

Acknowledgements   5

1. **'To Whom it May Concern'**   9

2. **The Options**   11

   Income 11; Deductions 15; Unemployment and social security
   16; National Insurance contributions 22

3. **Taxation and Accounting**   26

   Income tax 26; Capital gains tax 34; Value added tax 35;
   Accounts and their uses 36

4. **The Artist as a Small Business**   38

   Receptionist 39; Administration 40; Finance 41; Publicity 45;
   Design and technology 45; Information, training and business
   help 46; Archives 50; Legal matters 50; The artist as manager
   56; Employing staff 58; Personal welfare, health and insurance
   60; Unions and organisations for the self-employed 61

5. **Premises**   63

   Location 63; Is it legal to work at home? 64; Finding premises
   66; Lease or licence 68; Capital costs 69; Running costs 69;
   Buying and building 70; Specialist organisations 73

6. **The Product**   75

   Copyright 75; Registered designs 79; Patents 80; Trade marks
   80; Liability for your product 80; Safety in manufacturing
   processes 81; Insurance 82; Market trends 82; Technical
   development 83

7. **Marketing and Selling**   85

   Presenting yourself 85; Presenting your product 86; Use your
   expertise 86; Selling 87; Artists' agents 89; Selling abroad 90;
   Publicity 90

8. The Market Place   97

Professional galleries 97; How to approach a gallery 99;
Consigning work to galleries etc 100; Contract for an
exhibition 101; Touring exhibitions 102; Shops 103;
Alternative exhibition spaces 103; Festivals, fairs and markets
106; Outdoor sites 107; Competitions 108

9. The Financial Gap   109

Social Security 109; Collect money owing to you 109; Use a
professional skill 110; Part-time and temporary work 112;
Subsidy and sponsorship 113; Loans 113; Summary 113

10. The Art Subsidy Network   115

Services offered 115; National bodies 116; Regional and local
bodies 122; Sponsorship and patronage 129

Appendices   131

1. Useful Addresses   133

2. Further Reading   141

Index   145

Chapter 1

'To Whom it May Concern'

This book discusses self-employment as it applies to those who wish to spend most of their time on and aim to earn most of their income from the practice of their art, craft or designing. Many people contemplating this step will have undertaken a professional training at a college of art and design; the conventional careers to which such training can lead are not covered here. The book is intended to assist those who, by inclination or circumstance, are starting on a career in the visual arts as self-employed practitioners.

The usual reason that artists embark on this course is that the paintings, sculptures, photographs, videos, ceramics, clothes, costumes, jewellery, metalwork, glass, furniture, models, graphics and illustration cannot be made satisfactorily while they are in anyone else's employ but need privacy and self-determination. This presupposes that the artist in question (and 'artist' in this book will refer to the whole gamut of craftspeople and designers) has considerable self-confidence because it is a course best followed from determination and complete dedication.

The basic message of this book is that administrative skills can be learnt and that they will to an extent make a difference between business success and failure. (Artistic success or failure is quite another matter.) For example, those wishing to develop a successful business will find that it is necessary to understand public relations and be able and willing to learn extra skills quickly as circumstances demand. Often the artist who gets the commission is the one who can persuade a committee not only of the quality of his or her work but also that he or she understands the wider implications. John Dugger, who runs Banner Arts (which has moved to the USA) says, 'I began with an artistic vision, but things have flowed on from there. As soon as I started making large works for outdoors there were problems of water-proofing, installation, public liability, fire codes. I've had to learn how to present architectural drawings; I've had to learn costing and management and have become an expert machinist; I've had to learn formulae for calculating wind load on banners: I've had to learn to write specifications. I've had to learn about diplomacy and protocol.' (*Art Within Reach* published by *Art Monthly*, Arts Council and Crafts Council, now out of print but available at libraries.)

These skills may seem daunting and their necessity should not be underrated. But there are sources of help available for those needing or wishing to master them which can cover technical, organisational or financial requirements: there is the specialist help available from the national arts councils and regional arts associations, and establishments set up to assist small production enterprises such as the enterprise schemes and the RDC. Then there is the maze of agencies set up for specific purposes, such as the Law Centres, and many more that operate under mysterious initials such as AIR, SPACE, SHAPE, CAB, and LEntA, and it is this network that the book aims to unravel. The addresses of all these bodies, and others mentioned in the text, are given in Appendix 1 on page 133.

Two comprehensive surveys of artists and craftspeople (the Crafts Council's *Working in Crafts* and Gulbenkian Foundation's *The Economic Situation of the Visual Artist*) have compiled a lot of information about who the arts community is, what it does, where it does it and what it earns. They have established that a high proportion of practising artists are under the age of 40, that they do not earn much, and that women earn significantly less than men and have a lower rate of success in both job and grant applications. Therefore women's rights are discussed specifically, albeit briefly, but it is the rights, obligations and opportunities for everyone working in this field that this book aims to describe and clarify.

We are currently experiencing change and the result of change in our working and living environments and there are three particular areas that affect artists. One such change already achieved is the abolition of the metropolitan counties and the GLC, another is the new rules for claiming benefit under the Social Security Act of 1986 and the third concerns the changing role and responsibilities of the subsidy bodies. In addition to these, the Education Bill will affect artists who teach and the Poll Tax will affect us all. These acts will be reported as they occur in the national and specialist press and we would ask readers to incorporate them into the text of this book as appropriate. Figures quoted were correct at the time of writing, but readers are advised to confirm that they are still applicable.

Chapter 2

The Options

Everybody below retirement age in this country is classified as a potential worker unless the individual is receiving full-time education or is maintained by private means such as money, family or spouse. As a potential worker you will either be in someone's employ, be unemployed or self-employed. It is not generally recognised that you have to be one or the other although you can alternate between these situations or experience two at the same. But it is virtually impossible to opt out altogether because, in a tightly administered society such as ours, you can only avoid all bureaucratic attention if you have never been ill or educated or never claimed any social security benefits or ever worked.

Art is produced under heavy state subsidy: from the Department of Education (training and teaching) and then the Department of Health and Social Security (the dole) besides the accumulated budgets of all the national, regional and local subsidising bodies which, added together in the cold light of morning, are not insignificant.

This book does not intend to discuss the desirability of this situation or advocate any challenge to the 'system' or, more accurately, the dozens of systems that control employment, unemployment or self-employment. But how well you understand and make use of their different financial and legal requirements can affect your quality of survival and subsequently your self-determination.

Self-employment is the 'worker state' most usually adopted by artists and craftspeople so this will be discussed first.

Income

Life will not be simpler when you are self-employed but much, much more complicated. As a means of understanding what you will have to do, look at a pay slip from some conventional job such as teaching with a local authority: it will contain the details shown overleaf.

This is the 'Pay as you Earn' system and, once your employer has made all these deductions and you receive your net pay, that is yours to spend. The deductions and their amount are decided for you and there is no negotiation. It is simple and automatic.

Monthly pay slip

Basic pay (one-twelfth of your annual salary £
Supplements (such as an allowance for
unsocial hours) £_____

Deductions
Income tax (Schedule E) £
National Insurance contribution £
Pension £
Union dues £
Loans (such as a car loan) £_____

Net pay (which you actually receive) £_____

When you are self-employed, payment is not automatic at the end of the month whether you have worked well or badly, been sick or healthy; your basic pay may be very basic indeed and not arrive until months after you have earned it.

The same pay details as they pertain to an (imaginary) self-employed person's pay slip would be as follows:

Basic Pay (the agreed sum for your work) £
Supplements (these will not exist) £_____

Deductions
Income tax (this is a legal requirement) £
National Insurance contribution
  (this is a legal requirement) £
Pension (there is no requirement to pay this) –
Union (there are very few for the self-employed) –
Loans (any loans will be commercial) –_____

Net pay £_____

The other differences, invisible in this comparison, are that your pay will arrive (if you are earning anything at all) months after you have sold or done your work, you will on many occasions have to fight to get it, your income will probably be very irregular and, if you don't earn, you don't eat. No one will fight your battles or protect you and you can reasonably expect to spend several hours each week keeping accounts and records (administration) and looking after yourself.

On the positive side, you will not be hampered by unsuitable bosses or colleagues; although a lot of your work will be boring or hard, the point of it will be obvious; you will benefit from your own success and, hopefully, learn from any failure. While it is exhausting work it is also tremendous fun.

The legal requirements and best ways of coping with each item on that pay slip can be examined in turn:

Basic pay

What do you charge for your work? Generally, you charge as much as you can get and artists tend to overcharge for their work and undercharge for their time which is also a commodity to be rated properly.

Pricing of artefacts

Time. One principle of pricing items for sale, such as paintings, pots or tapestries, is whether the price you can get for them bears any relationship to the time you spend making them. Time is only one criterion; a contemporary tapestry would take several months to make, and some modern sculptures made of natural wood only a few days but that is the accident of their form and need not obviously reflect the experience of their creators. Whistler was accused of 'flinging a pot of paint in the public's face' and he admitted that one of his *Nocturne* paintings had taken only a few hours but that the price was also to pay 'for the knowledge of a lifetime'. Time is only one factor in deciding price and there are two sorts of time. There is the time it actually takes to make an item and there is the time of a working day that includes buying and preparing materials, cleaning tools, making coffee, answering the phone and going to the bank. If you cannot succeed in selling your full working day priced by the hour, the same as you would pay a garage mechanic or a typist, then either you must subsidise yourself in some way, speed up, or do something else.

Materials. Another factor bearing on the price you charge will be the cost of the materials from which your artefact is made plus presentation, framing, packaging and transport. There is also the cost of paying for and running your studio, of which a suitable proportion should be included in your price.

Reputation and exclusivity. Once you have any sort of reputation, you can put your prices up as there is no snobbery like art world snobbery. One article in a Sunday colour supplement or a TV interview and you can increase your asking price. However, if your work is selling well, it is

13

important to watch for the possible passing of your vogue, and maybe adjust your style or your prices accordingly.

How much do you want to get rid of it? Many young artists tend to price their work far too high and end up with piles of unsold work with yellowing price tags taking up expensive space. They might be better off with humbler prices, a happy public and a growing reputation.

What can your buyers afford? Depending on where you show your work, you will know your likely buyers. In London, Hyde Park railings or a stall at Camden Lock attract lots of passing trade; mixed art events such as the Contemporary Art Fairs or national competitions like the John Player Portrait Awards attract serious buyers. If you are accepted for these, get hold of the previous price-list, relate your work to similar work and add the annual rate of inflation for the number of years that have passed. A good gallery with a supporting catalogue is different again but be aware that some of the most prestigious purchasers, the public collections, have experienced serious budget cuts.

Gallery sales. If an established gallery accepts your work, take their advice on what you should charge; while even the most experienced cannot foresee what will sell, they know what prices clients will be likely to pay. If you establish a stable arrangement with a good gallery who start to act as your agent, do not undermine them by selling cheaply from your studio. They may make a proviso to this effect and if you contravene it, they are bound to find out.

Other price factors. The price you decide to charge for your work must have added to it: VAT (if you are registered – see pages 35–6), agent's fee and VAT and, if you deal through a gallery, their commission which can vary from 10 to 100 per cent. If you sell all over the country and from different outlets, you might find yourself altering your price, charging more in affluent, free-spending areas, and less elsewhere, so that your own average receipts do not alter too much.

Pricing your time. It might be to your advantage to spend quite a lot of unpaid time running a professional group, studio or gallery, but if you are asked to organise a group show, give a talk, take photographs or videos, make or design something for an outside body for which they could clearly pay, then you should price your time like any other professional. To underprice your experience and expertise presents your profession in a bad light. The current rates for further education lecturers are a good starting point for an hourly or daily rate plus local authority rates for travel and subsistence. You will be respected (and possible even paid!) if you present a professional attitude with a realistic valuation of yourself.

Deductions

Income tax and National Insurance contributions

Of all the unfamiliar facets of your self-employed life, these may well be the most unwelcome and daunting. They would also best repay your attention and the realisation that the payment of income tax and National Insurance contributions are legal obligations for neglect of which you can be prosecuted. Income tax for the self-employed is one of the most important subjects dealt with in this book and Chapter 3 is devoted to it. Don't try to evade National Insurance but read all about it on pages 22–5.

Union dues

One purpose of a union is to represent its members in negotiating pay and conditions and to protect them from the ills that are inherent in a working life. While there are some unions for sections of the art profession, their political influence is not remotely comparable with that of the unions affiliated to the TUC but neither do they operate a closed shop. There are a number of professional bodies listed in Appendix 1, membership of which can carry benefits but basically the situation is that when you work for yourself, you fight your own battles and win your own conditions. Further information is given on pages 61–2.

Pensions

One thing a union can negotiate is pension rights but with no union and no single employer, all you will be entitled to is the state pension, provided your NI contributions are in order. This need not concern you when you are in your early twenties, but when you are established and realise that youth does not last forever, you can select a pension scheme for the self-employed of which there are several widely advertised. The later you leave it, the more it will cost you for the same benefits at 60 or 65, which will be in addition to the state pension.

When you leave conventional employment you can, in some instances, cash in your local authority pension and the surplus contributions left after you have rejoined the state scheme are repaid to you. If this is not permitted, the amount you have paid in is 'frozen', to be released as a tiny supplement to your state or other pension when you reach retirement age. This depends on your remembering that it is there and no one will remind you of a few pension pounds sitting in the account of a long-forgotten employer.

Loans

One advantage of conventional employment is the 'perks' that go with it which can range from an advantageous car loan to the use of the office photocopier. Even a loan will probably be on favourable terms and be repaid painlessly by instalments each month from your salary.

When you are self-employed there are no perks and money is a commodity to be bought like anything else. Hence the rate of interest payable on loans has such prominence in the national and international news as its fluctuations will cost or save countless people a lot of money. The business of loans is dealt with in more detail in Chapter 4.

There is one further set of concealed differences between the comparative safety of a conventional employer and the independence and alleged glamour of the self-employed life; to give them alliterative neatness they are the Premises, the Pay, the Materials and the Motive. It may seem self-evident that an employer is responsible for the first three but to depend on self-motivation over the years when it is sustained by nothing except your self-faith, it must be sturdy indeed. Isolation, loneliness and financial insecurity will be your experience and there is no easy solution.

Income tax, pensions and loans relate both to employment and self-employment. There is a third state, unemployment, which also has important financial implications. You can be employed for part of your working time and self-employed for the rest of it, but you cannot (or shouldn't legally) be unemployed at the same time as well. It is a state strictly exclusive of the other two and bears some explanation.

Unemployment and social security

Most western countries have some form of social security which is what it says, a system whereby workers pay into a fund which is then available for those in need. In the United Kingdom, our social security system is fed by the National Insurance contributions and income tax and the payment of these is obligatory for nearly all workers, whether employed or self-employed.

Social security as we now know it was introduced in 1947 on the basis of a report by Lord Beveridge and was designed to offer protection from 'cradle to grave' from the worst ills of poverty.

For the first time since its inception, the Social Security Act of 1986 has introduced some changes and these are mainly to do with the system of assessment and amounts awarded. At the time of writing (summer 1988) certain of the terms and details of this Act are still under discussion, but the basis of the social security system remains the same.

This system operates by a series of benefits which are explained in a series of over 50 leaflets which are available singly from your local DHSS office or in quantity from the *DHSS leaflets* office. (Since July 1988, the DHSS has been separated into two departments and the social security arm will be known as the DSS, but the term 'DHSS' will continue in use for some time and will therefore continue to be used in this book.)

Some of these leaflets are simply redated versions of the old, navy and white leaflets with silhouette pictograms, but several of the most important leaflets have been reillustrated and rewritten to explain new rules. There is even a new social security logo which is like a dog collar without the dog in it and the lettering is arranged in natty perspective. But before you send for all these leaflets, you could first collect *Which Benefit? (FB2)* and then *Self-employed? (FB30)* or even *Employed or self-employed? a guide for tax and national insurance (IR56/N139)*.

While most of these leaflets are well-written, they are nevertheless presented by people who understand the system thoroughly and who are explaining a mass of complex detail of exemptions and exceptions that may remain less than crystal clear to the reader. In addition, some of the simplest questions do not have simple answers but are a matter of degree and interpretation as with the question, 'Is it legal to work from home?' (see Chapter 5).

In the context of this book, benefits such as War Pensions or Vaccine Damage will probably have little relevance, so the following information concentrates on those that are most likely to be of help to the self-employed artist.

All these benefits are divided into three categories:

- *Contributory benefits* for which you must have made a certain number of National Insurance contributions.
- *Non-contributory benefits* which are available to anyone in relevant circumstances.
- *Means-tested benefits* which are calculated by your current financial circumstances.

Contributory benefits

To be able to claim contributory benefits you must have done what the name says, 'contributed' a certain number of National Insurance contributions (NIC) and this is usually (there are exceptions to everything) calculated over 52 weeks.

'Starting credits' (as they are called) are awarded to everyone up to the age of 18. After the age of 18, you are either bound to earn them or you are exempt from buying them if you are a full-time student. If, for example, you work and earn during the holidays, you can choose to buy

17

them and this will be to your advantage later if you claim contributory benefits, but you are entitled to exemption while training.

For the complexities of National Insurance contributions see pages 22–5 but basically the rule is that only the law-abiding who buy their contributions can qualify for the following and not always then. Read on.

There are many other contributory benefits (they are the largest category of benefits) but these four are the most relevant:

Unemployment benefit
This benefit has four eligibility criteria of which only one relates to contributions; they are that:

1. You have paid (*or been credited with some of*) 52 weeks Class 1 National Insurance contributions. This is the class paid by the employer and the employee jointly and you cannot buy it on your own.

   You may be eligible for unemployment benefit if you have only bought some of these 52 weeks contributions and had the rest credited to you. For example, if you started your higher education course before you were 21 and have bought a set number of NI contributions by doing holiday work, you may qualify.

   This is why, even as a student, it is worth knowing exactly where you stand regarding your NI contributions and making sure that when and if you have a holiday job, you find out whether your employer is buying your Class 1 contributions.

2. You are capable of work by being well, strong and sensible. (If you become ill or injured while you are claiming unemployment benefit, it will be replaced by sickness benefit and possibly also income support.)

3. You are genuinely unemployed. If you are doing any of what social security staff call 'remunerative work' such as sculpting or painting for possible profit one day, it is wisest to tell them because it may affect your benefit.

4. Your availability for work is genuine.

Unemployment benefit is now a set amount and no longer related to the wage you earned in your last job. Also, it is payable for one year only, after which you have to apply for income support if you are still unemployed. This is well explained in a leaflet *Unemployed? (FB9)*.

The amount that you are paid on this benefit relates to the number of contributions that you have paid over the years and also to your situation, whether you have dependents or not etc. Like income support, it is taxable, and therefore must be declared as income. It provides a weekly cash payment for one year.

Statutory sick pay
This is only payable to employees and therefore will probably not concern the hero or heroine of this story.

Retirement pension
If you go in and out of conventional employment it is as well to remember that your retirement pension is assessed on your contributions and you could decide to keep up your (appropriate) payments.

Sickness benefit
This carries its own complex category of eligibility and exclusion, depending on your level of contribution in the previous 12 months.

Non-contributory benefits
These are benefits that are available without any NI contributions and they are not means-tested either. They are the category of benefit that appears to have been reduced by the Social Security Act, but the best known is child benefit that continues to be paid universally to rich and poor alike.

Means-tested benefits
The most widely claimed of these are family credit and income support (which has replaced the old supplementary benefit). They are not mutually exclusive and, under some circumstances, you can claim both. Both are dependent on your degree of financial need and you cannot claim them if you have between £3000 and £6000 in savings; there are so many qualifications on claiming these that it is pointless to list them, but they are clearly explained in the leaflet *Bringing up children? FB27*.

Another means-tested benefit is housing benefit that is claimable from the local authority by those on low income who have to pay rates and/or rent.

Income support
The Social Security Act replaced the old supplementary benefit with a new fund, income support. The main difference between income support and unemployment benefit is that the latter is dependent on your National Insurance contributions and the former on the level of your need. The main difference between the old supplementary benefit and the new income support is that supplementary benefit used to be paid in advance and income supplement is paid in arrears. For those who have current, urgent hardship, extra payments can be made under Crisis Loans from the social fund.

That, according to the rule book, is the main difference between the old and the new fund, but in reality the main difference seems to be that young, educated applicants will not so easily be able to rely on income support as a basic source of income as they did on supplementary benefit.

Income support is designed to meet the gap between what you have and what it is assumed you need. The application form itself is subtitled 'Help for people without enough money to live on'. Whereas the old supplementary benefit form enquired into your circumstances and environment, the new assessment form concentrates far more on your financial circumstances and availability and eligibility for work. Everyone applying for income support has a personal allowance (an amount which is automatically awarded to them) and this is assessed by finances, age and marital status. Then there is premium for special circumstances like dependants and disability and the two together add up to what is actually awarded.

However, the crucial question that arises with the new system as often as with the old, is whether it is legal to claim income support while doing your painting or pottery all the hours God sends. To claim it while working away on your 'thing' is actually using it as an interest-free source of money while you chase elusive fame, and, strictly speaking, it may be illegal.

Artists and those who work in a similar way (such as writers or composers) have been refused income support on the grounds that they are engaged in full-time 'remunerative work'. This is a *Catch 22* situation as the artist/writer/composer in question will have convinced the Inland Revenue that he or she is a professional and not a mere hobbyist (see page 27) only to have income support refused on the grounds that he or she is professionally producing work for reward, even though no one may be actually paying for it.

Artists can work for months or years without anyone buying their work (or ever, it has been known!) but this is still held to be 'remunerative' by the DHSS. Their logic is that work done full-time and intended for sale is remunerative work. The fact that it remains unsold is immaterial and what is important is that it is intended for sale. Income support cannot be (or should not be) used as a convenient source of interest-free income on which to build up a stock of work.

You are permitted to work up to 24 hours a week while drawing this benefit and this 24 hours is a full assessment of your involvement. If you are actually working on your painting or pottery, the 24 designated hours must include all the time you spend in work preparation, shopping for materials etc. The obvious question is who checks whether it is 24 hours or 130 that you work on your thing? The answer is that no one will probably check unless there is reason to suspect fraud, and how would any check be made? Someone hiding opposite to check the number of hours your studio light is on? This reply is an assumption tested by both time and officialdom.

Social security staff are as human as anyone else (usually) and become exasperated not by the odd artist struggling to survive but by the third generation claimants with every apparent intention of fraud, or those who repeatedly refuse to apply for job vacancies of which they are notified. If an obviously working artist claims benefit for a limited period of time and does not flaunt his or her continuing work and commitment, there is unlikely to be the staff or will to prove fraud, though fraud it is, strictly speaking. This is the situation as far as it has been defined but it is not for nothing that social security has been called the 'poor man's Arts Council'.

Also, there is one condition of claiming income support which could be inconvenient. It is that you are 'available for work' and if you are busy doing creative work, this might reasonably throw doubt on your availability. It has happened that social security officials have visited an artist's community studio to check how many of them were drawing benefit, which several were. The artists argued that, as the studio had a phone, they *were* available for work and this was apparently on this occasion allowed.

However, it must be pointed out that, under the new rules, when you sign on you agree to 'actively seek work and to be available to start a job that you are offered and which you can "reasonably" be expected to do'.

The aim of this reform was to reduce dependency on social security. Nevertheless, one suggested solution is as follows. When you leave art college with no job, no money and nothing but a huge appetite matched by a huge talent, sign on and claim income support. Similarly, if you are launching out into self-employment and things do not work out at once, sign on. If you are not financially supported by, for example, a spouse, but you are ostensibly a working member of society and you are not working for someone else, then you must either sign on or buy your own contributions as self-employed. Income support will credit you your contribution by official 'franking' (unless you are a single parent, in which case another system takes over); one way or another that contribution must be paid or you can be fined and made to pay the backlog. Then, when or if you start to earn, declare it even though this will alter your allowance and, when you earn enough to sign off, take over the purchase of your own contributions. You may need to sign on again at a later date if times are bad but the message is to come clean, declare your circumstances truthfully and make sure your contributions are bought or franked in an unbroken line. They are a legal requirement for all workers and will entitle you to some but not all, as it depends on the class of contribution, of those contributory benefits.

It is officially acknowledged that thousands of pounds are left unclaimed by those entitled to benefits and the reasons are clear: the complexity of the rules, the morass of qualifications, the (sometimes) poor quality of the explanatory leaflets plus the often inaccessible DHSS offices require both a logician to understand and an athlete to find. You are not alone if you find it all puzzling but as an energetic member of society, you should be able to do your homework before asking for the relevant help you need.

This relevant help can be sought from your local DHSS office or you can ring the freeline that offers advice on all social security matters. If you dial 0800 666555 between 9am and 4.30pm, Monday to Friday, you will automatically be put through to one of ten advice centres that cover the country. It can take some time to be answered but their advice is worth seeking, so hang on.

National Insurance contributions

The purpose of these is exactly what the name says, the nation's insurance against the worst effects of poverty, sickness and want. You legally have to buy your contribution or have it credited to you if you are working or looking for work unless you earn a very low income in which case you are exempt (£41 per week in 1988-89). If you are not working in what is called 'the employment market', for example, if you are a mother with young children or a kept spouse, then you will not be required to buy these contributions, but neither will you be eligible for contributory benefits, and your retirement pension (which may seem far off) will be adversely affected.

Therefore, if you are or aim to be a worker, the contributions must be bought and once you get this organised it will be an element in your campaign to have your status as a self-employed artist endorsed by those that matter. You can buy your contributions in one of two ways. Either you can go to the DHSS office and buy them every month or so or you can buy them by banker's order in which case you do not have a card but the purchase is recorded only in the stomach of some computer. If you buy the stamps which represent your contribution and actually stick them on your card, this can be comforting in that you can actually see them and you can also insist on a receipt as apparently the stamps themselves are no receipt of their purchase. This process avoids all future dispute as otherwise proof of your purchase depends only on your bank statement. However, if you trust banks, the latter system has its advantage in that, once a debiting order is made out, if the rate changes the new amount will automatically be debited to your account.

There are four classes of NI contributions and they are:

Class 1

If you are in conventional employment, these are the contributions that will be bought by you and your employer jointly. The amount you both pay will depend on how much you earn as it is earnings related. The contributions are deducted from salaries at source and sent to the Inland Revenue by the employer.

Class 2

These are the contributions you buy if you are self-employed unless you have been granted an exemption because your earnings are too low. Class 2 is a flat rate (£4.05 per week in 1988-89; it is a set amount that is only altered by Parliament in the Budget) and if you are employed for part of your time, you will pay Class 1 as well. Artists are actually specified in the NI 41 DHSS leaflet as an example of a profession likely to be buying this class of contribution.

Class 3

You can choose to pay Class 3 simply in order to benefit from contributory benefits if:

- You have been exempted from paying Class 1 because your earnings are so low;
- You are not liable at all because you are not a worker;
- For one reason or another your contribution record is not good enough to win your right to contributory benefits and you want to make it up so as to qualify.

Class 3 is also a flat rate and, because they are not compulsory, they are known as voluntary contributions. They have only one purpose, which is to safeguard your pension.

Class 4

You have to be doing very well to be required to pay this class. If your annual profits (not your turnover) from self-employment are over £4750 (1988-89), you will have to pay Class 4 which is not a flat rate but is a percentage of your profits (currently 6.3 per cent). Once or if you qualify for this, you really will not mind. Class 4 cancels out Class 2 but not Class 1 if you are still working for an employer. It is paid to the Inland Revenue.

Explanatory leaflets

The ins and outs and apparently endless rules for qualification and disqualification for the benefits versus contributions are explained in several DHSS leaflets which are surprisingly difficult to obtain and their distribution is acknowledged to be faulty. How well they are written and how helpful varies a lot but the key ones are:

NI 12   *Unemployment benefit*
NI 27A   *People with small earnings from self-employment called 'small earnings exemption'*
NI 41   *National Insurance guide for the self-employed*

The numbering of these leaflets appears to have no logical sequence to the public; sometimes classes of contributions are called 'grades' and these terms are interchangeable. But the main point is that if you are in the employment market you must buy your contribution unless you are exempted by low earnings, and to buy them in whatever class entitles you to contributory benefits. Or rather, it does if you have enough of them, and this is usually (but not always) 52 consecutive weeks with no gaps.

Credited contributions
If you are self-employed and fall on hard times, you can sign on for social security and for that period you will be officially unemployed and not self-employed. You will not be able to claim unemployment benefit unless you have 52 weeks of Class 1 contributions paid up and you will not have this if you are normally self-employed. So most readers of this book will probably fall back on income support.

The advantage of signing on is not only the money to tide you over but also that income support will 'credit' you with your contributions; the DHSS do not actually buy them but they credit them to your record as if they were bought. This will therefore keep your NI record intact and entitle you to some contributory benefits although not all of them.

Therefore, reasonable advice on the matter could be as follows: if you normally pay Class 2 contributions because you are self-employed and then hard times compel you to claim income support, cancel your own purchase of contributions as they will be credited to you. You can save the cost of them for this unemployed period but bought or credited they must be.

In conclusion, the following observation could be made. The quality of DHSS leaflets since the Social Security Act is greatly improved, both in language and layout. But the mass of rules and exclusion clauses is daunting; nearly every condition seems to be qualified by the word 'may'; for example, 'You may have to pay income tax on any income support payments you get'. The most confusing seem to be those benefits concerned with accident, sickness and maternity; applying for maternity benefit can be quite baffling.

There is now clearly a far greater requirement to seek and find work

- any work and not just work for which you think you are suitable. The penalties for giving false information or concealing illicit earnings are severe, and, all in all, to apply for and receive social security for any length of time is depressing and invasive of your privacy. So, while it can reasonably be regarded as a safety net if the worst comes to the dreadful, the remainder of this book looks at ways to maintain an income that may be more fulfilling and creative.

Chapter 3

Taxation and Accounting

This chapter will deal with tax and suggest how you can get the best out of this unavoidable system.

Income tax

This is a complex subject and whole books are devoted to it. Some of those concerned with artists' tax are listed in Appendix 2, but here the aim is to give the basic information so that you can at least start work with your tax situation understood and organised.

Of all the new and unfamiliar facets of your self-employed life, this may well appear to be the most unwelcome and daunting but some understanding of the tax system could reconcile you to its inevitable domination of your financial life. Income tax was originally introduced to finance the Napoleonic Wars and has been in force (with some twentieth-century refinements) almost ever since because it is effective. The Board of Inland Revenue deals with all aspects of income tax (which is direct taxation) and the Board of HM Customs and Excise deals with indirect taxation, such as VAT.

The Board of Inland Revenue has three 'arms'; the Inspectorate who inspect, the Collectorate who collect and the Inquiry Branch who inquire into large-scale problems; small-scale matters are dealt with by the Inspectorate. There are also the Commissioners who receive any complaints against the Board and hear appeals against its decisions. The country is split into 750 tax districts and each district has a Senior Inspector whose duty it is to send out tax return forms at the beginning of the financial year which starts on 6 April, so you should arrange your accounts accordingly. Each Senior Inspector has considerable discretion in assessing individuals' taxes and if you do not receive a long brown envelope in the first springtime of your career, do not be smug and suppose you have been overlooked, for the Inspector will track you down and inspect you in the end. It is your obligation to tell your Inspector what you do and where you are but if you don't, you will not escape.

The tax form that you will inevitably receive is folded into three like a medieval triptych. Once you have filled it in as best you can and returned it to your Inspector, you will receive another brown envelope which contains your tax assessment. If you are working for an employer and are on PAYE this will not offer many surprises, but if you are aiming to stand before your Inspector as a full-time, professional, self-employed artist, he may not endorse your stance. He may say that your claim to be a self-employed artist is not justified and he cannot allow your list of expenses to be set against your tiny income. In this case, you will be taxed on the gross income and so pay more than you would if expenses were allowed.

You may then remember that in the days when you were still making and selling pots from your half-converted garage or perhaps at your college show, you sold a piece of work to a friend and gratefully pocketed the cash. The cash was useful but the sale bought you no credit. Your Inspector might be more inclined to accept your artists' status now if he was aware of this and other sales, but when it has been unrecorded and only concluded by the handing over of greasy fivers, who is to know? And that other sale to the local bank which was paid for by cheque but kindly cashed by a neighbour – the Inspector will be aware of it from their accounts but where is it in yours? This is hardly professional behaviour and perhaps deserves to be rewarded with the tax status of an amateur.

Sales of work bring two benefits: the cash itself and the professional credit that goes with it. For your Tax Inspector to agree that you are what you claim to be will depend on your financial deportment.

Tax schedules

Income tax is divided into six schedules:

Schedule A. Income from rents.
Schedule B. Income from woodlands (abolished 6 April 1988, but tax relief for existing owners continues until 5 April 1993).
Schedule C. Public revenue dividends.
Schedule D. This is divided into six cases which are:

Case I   Profits from trade
Case II   Profits from profession or vocation
Case III Interest, annuities and discounts
Case IV Income from the UK not covered in Schedule C
Case V   Income from outside the UK
Case VI Annual profits not falling into any other case or schedule

Schedule E. Emoluments, wages, salaries and foreign earnings.
Schedule F. Dividends from companies in the UK.

Schedule E

The fees, wages and salaries taxed under Schedule E are those that you earn when you are under contract of service to an employer and enjoying some regularity of service. If you teach a regular set number of days for the Education Authority, you will be taxed under Schedule E, the tax due being deducted from your gross pay under PAYE. If you visit and teach for a single block of time, whether one or several days, then you should be paid gross and taxed under Schedule D.

Local authorities especially do their best to put all earnings straight on to Schedule E. If yours is but a single visit you can insist that as a condition of contract you are paid gross with no deductions. If they try and tell you that it is all the same in the end and makes no difference, this is simply the ignorant attempting to pervert the innocent. Why? Partly because under Schedule E you pay your tax immediately and under Schedule D you may not pay for 18 months or so, mainly because of the deductible expenses.

Take an example from the time-honoured profession of the artist, that of teaching. Suppose you teach in a school as a full-time art teacher and you teach, among other classes, a group of 30 12-year-olds to make terra-cotta piggy banks. You will certainly conclude that you need an overall and this you will almost just as certainly have to buy for yourself. Also, however near or far you live from school, you will pay for your own transport, and however diligently you study art and child development to become a better teacher, the costs involved will be met by you alone without affecting your already immutable Schedule E tax position.

Perhaps at the same time and in the same art department there is a visiting 'artist in school' appointed to work there for just one term. This appointee will be paid a gross fee from which no deductions will have been made and the artist concerned will also buy her own overalls, books, materials and transport as necessary but every item will be set against her earnings on the Schedule D tax form and affect the final calculation. This is the difference between Schedules D and E: on Schedule E there is very little negotiation and expenses cannot be claimed and on Schedule D you can claim all eligible expenses that are spent wholly in connection with your work. The narrowness of deductible expenditure is the characteristic of Schedule E and the breadth of opportunity for deductible expenditure the characteristic of Schedule D.

Schedule D and deductible expenses

Deductible expenses are those which you incur wholly and exclusively in pursuit of your trade or profession. These are running expenses, not capital expenditure, and they can include the following:

Premises. Studio (where rented or, if you work from home, a suitable proportion of your rent or mortgage). Running costs: rates, lighting, heating, repairs, cleaning. See capital gains tax on pages 34–5.

Materials. All creative materials (clay, paint etc), small tools, framing and presentation materials, protective clothing.

Studio usables. Cameras and equipment, film and tapes, bags and cases, shelves and storage units.

Office. Telephone, extensions, answering machine and portable phone, stationery, packaging, postage, printing, advertising, copying.

Other. Books, periodicals, newspapers, exhibition entrance fees, catalogues, travel, running a vehicle, accountants' fees. Before March 1988, entertaining foreign clients was also an allowable expense.

All these legitimately deductible expenses must be incurred solely in pursuit of your work. For example, if you are away from home doing a mural or putting up an exhibition, you cannot claim meals because you would have had to eat anyway, and no entertaining of clients is now claimable against tax.

Clothes also must be only to do with your work, such as protective overalls, and don't try to claim your jeans as these could also be used for casual wear – as the Inspector would say 'duality of purpose'. This duality is to be taken seriously; if you have a simple, four-roomed house of which the best and lightest room is the studio with one corner allocated as the office, legitimately you may claim a quarter of all your house costs against tax *but* this room should not also be obviously used as a guest room and sport a spare bed. But where an item is not shared in its purpose so much as shared in its time between work and your normal life, then a reasonable proportion may be claimed. The telephone is used for either work or private purposes and it might be reasonable to claim seven-eights (or some other clever proportion) of its cost as a deductible expense and the same sort of proportion for the car.

However, all these deductible expenses must be proved and here the necessity of organisation become clear. You must prove to your Tax Inspector that you have spent all you say on what you claim. Who is to believe that you have spent £500 on petrol and £300 on paints if you cannot prove it? The raw materials of such proof are:

Bills and receipts from your purchases listed daily in a
Diary showing day by day what you did and what it cost and then marshalled each month with receipts in chronological order into an
Expenditure book categorising and listing all expenditure and partnered by an

Income book listing all your income including income support and echoed by your
Paying in book with all the stubs filled in as are the stubs of your old
Cheque book saying exactly what everything was spent on and accompanied by
Receipts for rates, car repair, MOT, electricity, rent, telephone and all the other expenses which the self-employed life is heir to.

You do not need any fancy accounting system to marshal all this, just a spike on which to impale all your bits of paper and a few simple lined exercise books for your accounts. You must also allocate a few minutes each day and an hour or so each month to keep it all in order. Delay spells chaos, and chaos costs money you will not be able to afford.

If you do this each month, you will be able to add up your income and add up your expenditure, take one from the other and there is your profit (or loss). This is all a monthly statement is and it can be checked against your bank statements. After three months they can be added together to make a quarterly statement and then the four for the year can be totalled for an annual statement. It is no more mysterious than that. You will be taxed on your profit less your tax deductible expenses so it is in your interest to make your Tax Inspector believe they are as much as you say they are. It should be apparent that the list given of deductible expenditure is all for items that are expendable in running yourself and your studio; they are not for equipment or machinery, that is for capital items that are a one-off expense. Your kiln or your easel will be a capital item, your clay or your paint are deductible expenses, but small items that could properly be seen as capital items such as books, portable typewriters, tools and cameras are allowed as deductible expenses because they are comparatively small in value.

Your profit (or loss) is not the same as your turnover, which is the gross, whole, total amount of money that is paid to you for whatever purpose in a year, even if it is most or all or even more than all taken up in expenditure. It can be in your interest to make your turnover appear as high as possible because if you go for a loan or a mortgage, it is the turnover figure that lenders will use as a yardstick for the amount they will lend you. An example of how this can be done is as follows. Suppose that you take a painting for sale to a gallery and you want £100 for it; the gallery adds 50 per cent commission and it is sold for £150. In your accounts you can enter this as income of £150 and expenditure on the commission of £50. This will boost your turnover on paper but leave your profit of £100 truthfully recorded. This is called creative accountancy.

Schedules E and D together

Before education cuts removed many part-time jobs, a lot of artists and craftspeople taught for a few hours or days a week, working in their studios for the rest of the time. These same opportunities for a dual life are not now so frequent but it is still worth explaining the principle of being at once an employee and self-employed.

If you work for an employer under contract for a set and recurring period of time, you will pay Schedule E tax under PAYE. You could also be working as an artist the rest of your waking hours and claiming tax-deductible expenses against your profit (or loss) and paying tax under Schedule D.

But what if you don't make a profit, but a loss? Then the double advantage of your Schedule E job becomes apparent for not only does your regular work give you financial stability but you can offset a loss in your Schedule D business against your income in your Schedule E job. This is called carrying a loss *forward*. You can offset a loss against the income of your spouse or income from another source and this is called carrying a loss *across*. But you must choose to do one or the other – you cannot do both together – and to carry a loss across you must tell your Tax Inspector in writing.

You may wonder why you need to spend valuable time sorting out your accounts to prove that you made a loss when this self-evident state of affairs is not going to attract tax anyway. The reason is that a loss one year can reduce tax on profit the next year and third year after that. You are not allowed to make a loss indefinitely and the Tax Inspector will allow you three years of loss making before the Inland Revenue question your professionalism and qualification for Schedule D. This concession applies to sole traders and partnerships only; if you lose money in your own limited company, the loss can only be set against capital gains elsewhere, not against income tax.

Let us consider an example of profit and loss from an artist on Schedule D only.

Tax year		Profit/Loss	
		£	
1984–85		1000	Profit
1985–86	No tax paid.	2500	Loss
1986–87	No tax paid.	500	Profit
1987–88	No tax paid.	1500	Profit
1988–89	£500 remainder of loss from 1985–86 due for tax but it is taken up by the personal allowance; therefore no tax paid.	1000	Profit

31

The moral of this example is that if you can prove your losses, they can be carried forward year after year until they are used up, saving you tax on the way.

Suppose that you are on Schedule D and E because you have some teaching as well as your studio work. A typical tax return might show:

Tax year	Schedule E Income	Schedule D Profit/Loss	
	£	£	
1984–85	3000	2000	Profit
1985–86	3200	1000	Profit
1986–87	3500	2500	Loss
1987–88	3700	1000	Profit

The loss in 1986-87 was carried across to offset tax on the income from Schedule E. This artist could have chosen to carry it forward to offset next year's tax but it can be more advantageous to carry it across because if you carry it forward, the advantage may be swallowed up by inflation.

A development of these financial alternatives and a full explanation of the matter is given in the second of the Artlaw Guides *The Artist's and Craftsman's Tax Handbook* by David Binding. Like all Artlaw publications except the one on copyright, it is now out of print but it is worth tracking down a copy.

Regarding the taxation of married couples, the Chancellor made a declaration of impending change in the law in his Budget of 1988. 'The present system for the taxation of married couples goes back 180 years. It treats the income of a married woman as if it belongs to her husband. Quite simply, this is no longer acceptable.'

This Budget is the basis of the Finance Act now before parliament, and these and other changes are expected to be in force by 1990. At present, the Inland Revenue is exempt from the Sex Discrimination and Equal Pay Acts, but the new act will recrify this. However, under the present, discriminatory system, there are some benefits in that losses by one spouse can be set off against the earnings of the other. This is the result of being regarded by the Tax Inspector as one unit for the purposes of taxation.

The relief on tax by virtue of losses is only applicable where the candidate has been accepted by the Tax Inspector as a professional artist, able to claim tax deductible expenses. If you make a loss for too many consecutive years, this status will be questioned so you must not appear to be working without any expectation of profit.

Personal allowances and other tax exemptions

The personal allowance is a sum that everyone is allowed to keep tax free; for the year 1988-89 it is £2605 for a single person or married woman and £4095 for a married couple.

There are certain other exemptions from tax: for example, if you have any income from Savings Certificates or National Savings Bank investments bringing you interest, none of this is taxed unless your grossed up income brings you into the high tax bracket. But most important for the arts profession and the most likely difficulty to occur to the readers of this book is the tax exemption and liability on grants which are discussed below.

Making a loss

Making a loss is hardly a state that needs explaining but for the sake of completeness it is simply when your expenses exceed your income. Quite apart from how you live without starving, it is a state of affairs that your Tax Inspector will find particularly confusing. He is conditioned to believe that all work is done for profit; if your work does not bring profit, he will not understand why you go on working in an uncommercial idiom and he will not necessarily value your conviction, idealism or compulsion. It is indeed a clash of cultures.

If you are making a loss on your sale of work, you must be doing something to survive. Very few artists starve in garrets these days; they may quietly be suffering bachelor's scurvy in a badly converted room of a Victorian tenement while waiting for public taste to catch up with them, but meanwhile they will be surviving on one or more of the following:

Social security benefits: discussed in Chapter 2.
Alternative freelance earnings: discussed in Chapter 9.
An earning spouse: needs no discussing, just embracing.
Part- or full-time employment.

Taxation of grants etc

This situation regarding taxation of grants from the Arts Council, the Crafts Council and the regional arts associations is not clear but certain guidelines were agreed between the Arts Council and the Inland Revenue in 1979 that do stand as an accepted basis for agreement between clients and their tax inspectors.

All grants and receipts of that nature are now divided into two categories:

Category A – taxable
Commissions, grants, awards – whatever they are called, all these are basically money grants and are for a specific purpose or project or to meet specific expenses.

Category B – not taxable
Training bursaries in whatever field (this is an exception to the guidelines for Category A).
Any award for 'buying time' and unrelated to specific projects.

Other professionals such as writers, choreographers and composers have as much concern as artists to obtain guidance on this matter as they have a similar reliance on the Tax Inspector's decision. Further evidence of the uncertainty surrounding this subject concerns prizes won in open competition; the Whitbread Literary Award was confirmed as being not part of an author's professional income and therefore not taxable, but this decision only indicates any decision likely to be made by a Tax Inspector in the future about a prize and does not determine it.

This division of grants into Categories A and B stands as a guideline only to the tax position of grants given, for example, by an RAA and does not determine their status. If and when you receive a grant, ask whether the tax position has been clarified and, if not, try to ascertain to which category it pertains and then argue your own case. This national inconsistency confirms the old adage that if you laid all the bureaucrats from head to feet in a long line, they would not reach a conclusion, but in practice it is the case that 750 tax districts will have 750 opinions.

Capital gains tax

Capital gains tax is the means whereby the government taxes the increase in the capital value of your property. It is a matter for serious consideration by great property owners but in our context it has only one likely consequence.

The largest item of property that you are likely to buy and sell is your house. Suppose that you buy a house for £50,000 and, some time later, sell it for £74,000. Your profit or, in this context, your capital gain will be £24,000 but because it is your only house used for your exclusive dwelling purposes, it is exempt from capital gains tax. This particular tax is a way of discouraging people from owning property that they do not use in a time of housing shortage but also applies, subject to certain conditions, to sales of jewellery over £5000, shares and securities.

But you must still consider CGT if you have claimed your mortgage interest and running costs against income tax on the basis that you run your business from your home. Supposing that you have claimed one-quarter of these costs under Schedule D, you will then be compelled CGT on one-quarter of that profit, that is on £6000. But the annual exemption is £5000 (1988-89) so that cheaper properties escape the tax altogether.

If you live in London or own expensive property and so foresee the likelihood of having to pay capital gains tax, you can avoid it in the following way. Although you are entitled to claim a proportion of the cost of your house for your business, you will be exempt from tax if you do not do so. You can therefore 'let' yourself a room for about £25 per week and claim this against income tax as justifiable rent. If you have a spouse to whom you can pay this, it is easier, and if the house is your only home and you do not claim, you will not have any call to pay capital gains tax.

Value added tax

Value added tax is a tax for which we are all unpaid tax collectors for the government. It is a tax on the increase in value between the raw materials and the finished object; that is, the lump of clay and the finished teapot. It is a successful tax, hence its gradual encroachment on previously protected areas. The standard rate is 15 per cent at present. Any changes in its application are made by the Chancellor of the Exchequer on Budget day which is another reason to follow his speech as it can, by changing VAT, affect you at once.

The principle is that we all pay VAT on whatever we buy, unless it is exempt or zero rated (like books) but if you are registered, for VAT, you can claim it back, to an extent.

VAT is administered by the Customs and Excise and their local office is listed in the telephone book with their VAT department; they publish a leaflet called *VAT General Guide Notice No 700*. They or your accountant will guide you through registration (should you decide or have to do so) and there are two sorts of registration.

Voluntary. You can register at any time.
Compulsory. You have to register if your turnover exceeds a certain amount in any year or quarter and currently (1988-89) this is £22,100 pa or £7,500 in any calendar quarter. This is a recognised problem with what are called 'seasonal earnings' and there are accepted ways whereby their sudden payment need not make you liable for registration.

When you register for VAT you will then have to charge VAT on all goods and services and that is your 'output'. You will, whether registered or not, be paying VAT on what you buy like the rest of the population and the VAT on these purchases is your 'input'.

If the VAT you receive on your 'output' is *more* than that which you pay on your 'input', you have to pay the difference to the Customs and Excise. But if the VAT you receive on your 'output' is *less* than that which you pay on your 'input', then the Customs and Excise will pay you the difference. Once you are registered, the amount of VAT you pay and receive will be evened up whereas if you are not registered, you simply pay it like everybody else.

The advantages of registering are therefore obvious: you do not in the end pay VAT. The disadvantages are less obvious but they exist. Once you are registered for VAT and have your own VAT number you are required to keep detailed records of your purchases and sales and you have to send in your completed VAT returns every three months. This is a bookkeeping exercise that many find time-consuming and demanding and you are also subject to searches by the VAT officers who operate according to their own rules which can be inconvenient. This is not a horror story, but there is a body of them. The penalties for late payment are heavy. Also, once you charge VAT on your goods and services, that is your 'output', you can become unpopular with customers as they will then have to pay more, unless of course they are themselves registered for VAT. It is a bookkeeping hassle and many artists go to some lengths to remain unregistered.

It is therefore reasonable to advise that when you are getting established with your work, you forget about VAT but make sure that when you are owed a lot of money it is not all paid in together as they may take you over the magic 'three months limit' and you may find that you have to register simply because of one surge of income. However, if you have a lot of capital expenditure on large items like a kiln, you could find it worth your while to register and claim VAT back. At the end of your first year's operation, look at your VAT business expenditure (input) and compare it with what you would have made if you were registered and charging (output). If the difference is sufficiently in your favour, consider registration but do not underrate the accountancy involved. Your accountant can do it for you but you must supply impeccable records and he will charge.

Accountants and their uses

Most artists are not by inclination good at financial matters and many choose to buy themselves the services of an accountant. The benefits of this are that the accountant will speak the same language as the Tax Inspector (they will both know what emoluments are) and will argue your case from a position of professional equality; also, the accountant can advise you on tax deductible expenses, some items of which are borderline and some of which you may never have considered (one fabric designer successfully claims seeds for his garden on the grounds that he works with colour) and finally the accountant will be up to date with changes in the financial law and practices.

How to find an accountant who is sympathetic and understands artists is another matter. The best way to deal with this and other advice is to find someone in the same line of business as yourself but who is rather more advanced and ask who they use, or you can ask your bank, your regional arts association or the Rural Development Commission. Accountants are now allowed to advertise, as are solicitors and doctors, but it is the most expensive that can afford the most obvious advertisement, so a young, self-employed accountant just setting up may be your answer.

Many artists decide to use an accountant when it becomes clear just how complicated their income can be, but any accountant will charge according to the time spent on your affairs so it is in your interest to present orderly evidence of your activity. If you give your accountant a mass of fluttering bits of paper done up in an old table cloth with a safety pin, he or she will charge you for the time it takes to sort it all out. But if you offer a pile of neat receipts in date order and related accurately to your listed expenditure, the subtraction of this from your probably humble income to arrive at your profit (or loss) will probably not take long. And of all expenses, an accountant's fee is the most obviously tax deductible.

Chapter 4

The Artist as a Small Business

As soon as you establish your self-employed status with the professional world in general and the Tax Inspector in particular, you are a 'small business' with personnel (yourself), a product (to make) and a purpose (to sell it). In modern day parlance, Van Gogh was a 'small business', so was Gauguin, so was anyone who ever produced anything for sale, so it is not a term that will condemn you to philistine obscurity.

The legal obligation to pay income tax and your National Insurance contribution has been looked at in some detail, but that is only the start of the story. An analogy between your operation and a rather larger and more conventional business can illustrate the further requirements that self-employment will make of you.

Imagine a business of about 20 employees that produces sets of ornamental flying ducks that hang on the wall. Perhaps this firm has been moribund for years but, with the revival of 1950s nostalgia and a take-over by the founder's grandson, the ducks have met with a new lease of life. Imagine, if you will, that you have dealings with this business and so visit them in their premises, designer-posh in Milton Keynes, efficient but industrially swamped in Feltham, or derelict in Liverpool.

When you go into this factory, the first employee you see will be the *Receptionist* who asks you your business and who may double as *Administration* in which case she (and it is always a she) will be rattling away at a typewriter or else pattering away at a mellifluous word processor. As you pass down the corridor you will see the employees' names and departments on their doors and they will probably include the following:

- *Finance: accounts and wages* who know the current profit and loss situation of the firm, pay the wages and creditors, invoice goods despatched, chase debtors, and advise on what the firm can afford.
- *Publicity and public relations* who decide what sort of advertisement is cost-effective and whether conventional ducks should be aimed at the elderly or revamped ducks at the nostalgic nouveau jeune. PR present the business's image to the world.
- *Sales and export* who are responsible for making sales and organising exports.

- *Design and technology* who decide whether the ducks remain in fragile, heavy plaster or are redesigned according to modern, ornithographic observations and made out of fibreglass.
- *Information and archives* who have all the data on the earliest designs of ducks that the firm produced and information on anything that may be of use to the firm, such as details of rival ducks.
- *Legal adviser* who sorts out contractual problems and decides what to do about poor quality imitations sold for half the price.
- *The manager* who ultimately makes the decisions and endeavours to earn a living for everyone and profit for the shareholders.
- *Maintenance and cleaning* will do as their title says for the premises and equipment.
- *Stores* will buy in and hand out equipment and materials.
- *Workshops* are where the ducks are made.
- *Despatch* is a garage of fleet vans ready to distribute the ducks to nationwide outlets.

For simplicity's sake, this example is of an old-fashioned, paternalistic firm but the point of the example is that, while your product may bear no relationship at all to ducks flying up the wall, you yourself will have to be each employee in turn once you become a small business. You will be at the same time the accountant, the receptionist, the designer and the delivery driver. A lot of this work is common sense, but then most things are common sense when you know how. An early motorist once queried the bill of five guineas for putting right his new-fangled car and the mechanic said that it was five shillings for the spare part and five pounds for 'knowing how'. The aim of this book is to tell you how because the work you do as an artist will not be common at all; it should be extraordinary ... that's why the commonsense work is worth it.

Let us consider each role in turn and see how you can adapt to its necessity.

Receptionist

Unless you are resolved to make a career out of being objectionable (like Groucho Marx), good manners are amazingly important, as is a good telephone manner, which consists of speaking clearly and to the point. Whatever else you economise on, a telephone is essential, with a pen and pad beside it. A mobile phone is useful and an answering machine will mean that no opportunity that comes your way is left unanswered. Also, you will be expected to be available and enthusiastic at all times, as are vicars; other professionals can go home, you can't.

Once you are a professional in business, you will be subject to all sorts of visits at your studio whether you advertise it or not. Planning officers, accountants, arts association officers will all have dealings with you sooner or later, local journalists will come round looking for controversy and hopefully potential clients also. Most visits will be planned in advance but some will not, so try to keep a room or part of an area in your studio less chaotic than everywhere else. Many of these visitors will be making many such visits so try to provide a comfortable chair with an offer of a cup of tea, turn off the radio and give them your attention. A light desk to view slides, some work on display and a business card are all appropriate.

Adminstration

Organisation is essential unless you wish to work in confusion and squalor.

Letters. You will be remembered ultimately by your work but your first point of contact with the world will usually be your letter, and its quality can affect the speed with which your work becomes noticed.

The first rule for a business letter is to type it. The only acceptable exception to this is if you have really beautiful handwriting (in the Edward Johnston class) but even then you should consider the person who is to receive it. Typing is always more legible, it implies you have kept a carbon copy and modern businesses would no more send a handwritten letter than they would write it with a goosefeather quill. The era of word processors is here and catalogues, research and books are increasingly relying on them and, once you are familiar with a typewriter keyboard, you will be better able to use a computer keyboard.

As you join the brimming art market, regard your letter as your ambassador. Your name and address should be clear with a postcode and phone number for day and evening and the letter should be correctly addressed to its recipient. The content should be unambiguous and it remains a sad truth that the quality of the letter dictates the quality of response. Some notes on letter writing are given on pages 67-8.

This also applies to your *curriculum vitae* which you will need to include with many of your letters and applications. This is a brief outline of your educational and professional history, usually laid out on one side of your headed paper. It should include all your personal details such as age and secondary education, then an account of your higher or further education if you completed it, and an account of your work experience. Any other details that are of professional relevance such as an apprenticeship, any scholarships, grants or prizes should be included and any pursuits or interests that indicate your abilities. Your curriculum vitae means that the accompanying letter need not explain who you are and what you do as all that information is neatly encapsulated on a separate sheet. It should, of course, be typed perfectly, and it is acceptable to send out good photocopies. Retain the original.

The letter paper that you use need not be expensive but it must be memorable and it should imply your aesthetic nature. It need not have a watermark but somehow try to have a headed paper – a small lino print done in the kitchen with a spoon, anything – and lay the content out well. One artist carved her initials with lino-cutting tools on to a shoe heel bought from a heel bar, and fixed it on a piece of wood to use as a stamp. While it is tempting to use coloured paper, it has two disadvantages: it is difficult to make corrections on it and it does not photocopy very well. You can use colour for your envelope and one craftsperson makes envelopes out of cheap coloured paper with pinking shears that are miracles of origami and are impossible to ignore.

Filing. All small businesses evolve their own filing and administration system but just before you file all your papers under 'E' for Everything, remember that losing things costs time and temper and both are commodities you will not be able to squander.

Finance

The main financial undertakings in a small business have already been discussed in Chapter 3, namely tax, National Insurance, VAT and the use of an accountant. But there are other aspects of this important matter which cannot be ignored.

Banks

It is difficult even to start a business without some initial capital to buy the essential materials and equipment. Unless you have private means, this capital will have to be earned or borrowed. Some artists earn it by doing a hard job for a short time, such as driving a lorry to Greece and back, or you can apply for a loan.

Loans

You can go shopping for money as for any other commodity. The sources of borrowed money can be:

Family. Nice if you've got it.
Friends. Do agree clearly the terms of any loan and write them down, such as the interest or lack of it, the length of time, rate of repayment.
High street banks. This is possibly the source least likely to cause you trouble.

The most usual place to apply for a loan is one of the high street banks and you can go shopping for a bank by looking at their publicity leaflets and finding out if they appear to favour small businesses. Then make an appointment to see the manager; these days it is less likely to be the local branch manager than one of several managers responsible for a group of branches, one of whom specialises in small businesses. While even bank managers may yearn to back a genius and bask in the reflected glory (and this has happened) such romantic daring has usually been bred out of them on their way up to becoming managers.

But there has recently been a noticeable and favourable change in the attitudes of the high street banks towards small enterprises in general and art and design schemes in particular. The written quality of their leaflets which describe their services are more inviting and clear, less sexist, discriminatory and hidebound than previously. It may or may not be relevant that Barclays has had all its leaflets illustrated by Ian Beck, although inexplicably he is not acknowledged.

Banks are in the business of making loans but any manager will need to be convinced of three things: that you have some surety against a loan, that you are a professional artist and that you will be able to keep up the repayments. Property can be a surety, or a relative or friend can stand as surety and will only be called on if your business fails absolutely. Your professionalism will be indicated by evidence of any sales of work (this is another reason not to make cash sales without paperwork), any reviews, grants or prizes that you have won and your ability to repay the loan will be assessed not only on your present income but also by the organisation of your business, whether your accounts are in order and how far you understand what is involved in setting up a small business.

Loans are made for fixed terms with agreed plans for repayment of principal and interest. An overdraft is a temporary arrangement to overdraw; it must be agreed by the bank beforehand and interest is charged only on the sum involved for the period of its overdrawing. It can therefore be cheaper than a formal loan. In theory, the facility can be withdrawn by the bank at any moment without notice, but unless you handle your account badly, this is not likely to happen.

Banks want to make a good investment for their money, not a bad one, and a cash flow forecast which shows what you need to earn and spend each month will help to convince them that you know what you are doing. If you get into difficulty, tell your bank manager and if you feel he is not sympathetic, take your account elsewhere.

Banks operate the government Loan Guarantee Scheme under which they are empowered to lend money to businesses who cannot offer the security that their stringent standards demand. The interest rate is higher than the bank base rate.

Cash flow

This is exactly what it says, cash coming in and cash going out, not only as it happens but as a forecast of what you expect to happen for the next six months or so. Assuming that you have a bank account, you should ask for a monthly statement and check each item, as even banks can make mistakes. It is better to know your own financial situation, however bad, than have the bank tell you as a surprise that you are overdrawn.

The complexity or simplicity of your financial accounting will partly depend on how much money you have coming in (your turnover) and how much going out (your expenditure) and how many transactions you make. If you are making hundreds of salt-glazed coffee mugs and selling from 20 outlets, your accounting system will have to be more detailed than if you sell one large painting every six months for the equivalent amount of money. Craftspeople will find the Crafts Council's book *Running a Workshop* particularly good for help on handling a lot of transactions; of the various accounting books that are available, the best are stocked by Rymans and W H Smith. But whether you take £2000 by selling 1000 mugs or one painting, the rule is that you know where your money comes from and where it goes to.

Chasing debtors

It is one thing to have money owing to you and quite another to receive it. One of the ways given in Chapter 9 to fill a financial gap is to retrieve money from your debtors. There are different sorts of debtors:

Local authorities and large companies

Organisations such as these will have large and complex financial departments dealing with hundreds of transactions and they will generally take some weeks to pay an invoice. They may or may not have a deliberate policy of keeping small accounts waiting but the result is often that their delay can cause cash flow problems for the small business.

Suppose that you sell a painting to a large brewery or complete a short 'artist in schools' residency for an education authority, in both cases for a set and agreed fee. First, you show you are a professional by sending an invoice which is a request for payment. Address it correctly, quote the agreed price and then wait. After one month send a statement, pointing out how much is outstanding. After six weeks send a courteous letter to the person who engaged you and ask for payment. After two months send another statement with a copy of the invoice and another letter. After that, adopt other tactics. You are not allowed by law to threaten and it is unwise to be rude, but you can be persistent. Find out if the managing director or the Director of Education has a motherly secretary and keep phoning up at lunch time. You can write a brief letter to the head of the firm or organisation and ask for payment and this usually resolves matters. The electricity and gas boards wait five to six weeks before issuing a final demand and this is a reasonable period of time to wait. But if you are still left unpaid, you can resort to the small claims procedure at the County Court and warn your debtors that you are going to do so.

Many women who run a small business rightly suspect that they are treated especially badly on this matter of receiving payment.

Small organisations and individuals

Large organisations often don't pay for up to three months and it may be deliberate financial policy: similarly, small organisations and even individuals keep you waiting because they also can earn interest on the money they owe you, they may have cash flow problems or they may even be on the verge of bankruptcy. Do not expect altruism or honour over money, only self-interest.

Small claims through the County Court

All this presupposes that your contract is in perfect order and that there is no query as to who owes whom what. But, if you remain unpaid, wait the length of time that the electricity board and the gas board would wait, and then you can do one of three things:

- You can give up and if the amount of money involved is small, it is occasionally better to do so rather than make an enemy;
- You can repossess your work, but you must give adequate written notice that you intend to do so; or, again after adequate written notice;
- You can go to the County Court and initiate a *Small Claims Procedure* for any sum up to £500.

Court procedures have been considerably simplified to help those who run small businesses and have no legal knowledge to reclaim money or goods owing them without incurring the cost of a solicitor. The County Court deals with private disputes and claims up to £5000; you are unlikely to be concerned with the Magistrates Court, or the Criminal Court which tries criminal cases.

For small claims up to £500, there are no court proceedings and the case is heard in private by the registrar and you simply pay on a sliding scale. The minimum fee is £6. The defendant also has to pay some costs in addition to the debt so it is in his or her interest not to let matters get this far. The scale of charges for small claims is:

£60-£300 sum claimed or value of goods: 10p for every £1

£301-£500 sum claimed or value of goods: £35

For claims over £500 a court hearing is required, but for claims of up to £5000 it remains in the County Court.

£501-£2000 sum claimed or value of goods: £38
£2001-£5000 sum claimed or value of goods: £40

After £5000 it is no longer a 'small claim' but becomes a different legal category. There is an explanatory booklet issued by the Lord Chancellor's Department called *Small claims in the Country Court: How to sue and defend actions without a solicitor* that you can get from your County Court and it is well worth reading if you have problems. The County Courts are in the telephone directory listed under the county council and in the Yellow Pages under 'Courts'.

When you consider the time that you spend chasing debtors, it is worth taking steps to avoid the necessity for it. It is unrealistic to demand 'cash on delivery', for only emergency services like plumbers and vets can do that, but look at what other small businesses do. One normal, businesslike procedure is to offer a discount for prompt payment; this is not in fact a discount on the original price but a built-in, legitimate cost to cover the inconvenience you incur by having to wait for your money. Local authorities and other large institutions may, justifiably, be asked for a cash payment in advance for materials and travelling expenses. If this is not forthcoming, see you put in an early claim for expenses and include one or two anticipated items, such as journeys that have not yet actually taken place, and then pay your costs by credit card.

Do as you would be done by
It will be your decision whether or not to treat your creditors as badly as your debtors will probably treat you. It is not the purpose of this book to give ethical advice (and one definition of an ethic is that it is like a moral only bigger), but to become known as an honest and caring dealer might be of more benefit in the long run that the reverse.

Publicity

This is covered in Chapter 7 'Marketing and Selling' where its discussion is more appropriate.

Design and technology

You are already your own designer and appropriate technology should by now be integrated into your creative understanding. But one problem in a working life is solving technical problems and keeping up with technological developments – simply knowing about them and then having the time, money and opportunity to master them.

The professional periodicals are the best means of keeping abreast of aesthetic and technological developments in your specialism and for knowing generally what is going on. *Art Monthly* and *Arts Review* carry a lot of reviews and information, but for an alert newscaster of everything that is now, or is about to happen, *Artists Newsletter*, published every month, is a magazine no professional should be without. If you can arrange access to a good polytechnic or university library it is a good idea even if you only use it once a year to check up on back numbers of these and other magazines.

Information, training and business help

It is government policy to encourage small businesses and the self-employed as part of the current national change in work patterns. The Department of Trade and Industry is one part of this instrument for change, the Department of Employment and the Manpower Services Commission are others. These and other bodies offer various schemes and incentives that can benefit the artist but the main problem is the difficulty of understanding the terms and detecting the exclusion clauses before you apply.

Government publications from any department are characterised by one of two styles: either a formal jargon or, where a 'communication consultant' has clearly been employed, the graphics are attractive and the written material is presented in a cheerful way that suggests that this scheme will solve everyone's problems.

This cheerful style simplifies the presentation but not the raw material, and it is not only government schemes that are complex, for the administration of even the smallest business is both complicated and time-consuming. When the small business trader has the opportunity to speak, as on the Radio 4 *In Business* programme, the complaint is that the demands of VAT, tax, requirements of the health, environmental, fire, planning and building regulations officers erode time and energy from the business in hand.

The artist and craftsperson especially can find the setting up and running of a studio so onerous that there is no time for creative work. The only answer is to keep the business as simple as possible for as long as possible. Don't register for VAT until you have to; rather than employ full-time staff, rely on freelance help such as an accountant or typist, and when you look for these specialists, those who operate from their home address will be cheaper than those in business premises. If you employ help in the business, you have to operate PAYE unless you pay less than £50 each week and have to deduct National Insurance contributions from wages over £41 a week. Once you are established, you may be able to pay someone else to do the necessary administration engendered by employees.

Among the government schemes there are tailor-made opportunities for artists which they often ignore. Some of the most beneficial are described here.

Training Agency (formerly Manpower Services Commission)

The MSC was set up in 1974 to run public employment and training schemes when unemployment became accepted as a long-term or even permanent national condition rather than a temporary phenomenon. This well-known name has now been reorganised out of existence, and, under the Employment Act of 1988, the Training Agency has been founded which, with the Department of Employment, has taken over the MSC responsibilities.

The Training Agency is responsible for vocational education and training. The Department of Employment is responsible for employment. The Training Agency has its headquarters in Sheffield but it has 55 area offices covering the country under a smaller number of regional offices. Similarly, the Department of Employment has about ten regional offices, but the problem is to find them. Both organisations confidently say that they are listed in the telephone book, but this is only true for large cities. If you wish to find either organisation, phone directory enquiries, and when they ask which town, give the nearest large conurbation and ask for the relevant number. Be prepared to ask for the defunct MSC if they say they have no record of the Training Agency.

Of the various services that both bodies run, the most relevant to artists are as follows:

Jobcentres – run by the Department of Employment
There are over 1000 across the country and they have the current details of MSC schemes which do change their terms and conditions, so it is worth keeping in touch with them. Your Jobcentre will have details of any basic business training schemes, for instance.

Professional and Executive Recruitment (PER)
This advertises the availability of professional staff in all fields for conventional employment through the weekly *Executive Post* which is sent

to everyone listed on the Register. It might best be used as a means of finding well-qualified staff if and when you need them. This is to be privatised, but will fulfil the same function.

Community Programme – run by the Training Commission
This exists to employ adults on programmes that are of benefit to the community. Under the agency of the regional arts associations it has been used to supply assistance for public murals, sculptures and other works but as with all such schemes, there are strict rules for its implementation.

Enterprise Allowance Scheme – run by the Training Commission
The key to the EAS is that you must apply *before* you start trading. This does not mean that you will be disqualified for the odd few sales, but you must apply before you make any serious attempt to sell your work.

It was set up to help unemployed people establish a small business while drawing social security. Applicants must be over 18 years old, have been registered unemployed for at least 13 weeks, prepared to work full time and be able to raise at least £1000 capital to invest in their business. Eligible people are then allowed £40 per week for 52 weeks while they set up in business; it is paid fortnightly and is taxable.

Enterprise agencies
There are over 200 enterprise agencies across the country and they have been set up one by one since 1979 by local government with considerable sponsorship from local industry. To an extent they overlap the services offered by the Rural Development Commission as their aims are not dissimilar, but the RDC is for the English rural areas only and the enterprise agencies are for urban areas. In Scotland and Wales the development agencies fulfil the same role. The enterprise agencies have different schemes according to their locations but they all help small businesses, either with some operational aspect (for no small business is going to be good at everything) or else with a particular problem such as finance or premises.

The London Enterprise Agency (LEntA)
LEntA is the London branch of this network and it has made special provision for artists and designers. In 1985 it set up the Design Enterprise Programme whereby college leavers are invited to attend a course which gives them a grounding in the management of a small business. They also produce a booklet *A Business in Art and Design* that gives in a very brief version the same sort of facts and advice as this book.

Design Enterprise Fund

This is also operated by LEntA and is available to art- or design- based businesses anywhere within the Greater London area. It consists of interest-free loans up to £1000 and loans of 10 per cent up to £5000 for certain purposes. If funds are unavailable and, like all such schemes it is receiving too many applications, LEntA directs applicants to other sources.

Graduate Enterprise Programme

This programme consists of a series of courses run by polytechnics and universities for graduates, including art and design graduates. They are nothing to do with the enterprise agencies (it is a pity they use the same word), and since there appears now to be no central coordination of them, you must ask your local Jobcentre or institute of higher education whether such a course is run in your area.

Department of Employment

This department has taken the Small Firms Centres under its wing. Help is also available by telephone from 13 centres covering the country. Between 8.30am and 5.00pm Monday to Thursday and 4.30pm on Friday, if you dial 100 and ask for Freefone Enterprise you will find an advisory service ready to listen and advise. Well, you will if you can get through as it is a very busy service, but they also produce a series of well-written leaflets that are sent on request (they are listed in Appendix 2).

Rural Development Commission (formerly CoSIRA)

CoSIRA has lost its memorable name in a merger with the Development Commission to become the Rural Development Commission ('They can't leave anything alone, as Quentin Crisp observed when they invented the atom bomb that doesn't flash. Incidentally, does any reader also remember Quentin Crisp modelling for the life class at St Albans School of Art in the 1960s?) However, its aim remains the same, which is to promote jobs in rural areas. It still retains its central office in Salisbury to which all enquiries should be addressed. There are 31 Rural Development Commission – Business Service offices throughout the country and their definition of 'rural' and 'business' remains unaltered.

The Rural Development Commission was founded in 1909 to help counteract the decline of rural industry. It offers technical, informational and business help to small businesses – 'small' meaning employing fewer than 20 skilled people and 'rural' meaning in a designated area with under 10,000 population. The businesses it caters for are mainly those concerned with 'making or mending' and the help it can offer artists setting up as a small business is not insignificant.

The county branches of the RDC vary as do all branches of a central organisation but the best are excellent within their trading 'no nonsense' terms. They can help with premises, finance, materials, equipment or manufacture and an actual recent example of their help concerns an artist's need for a machine to cut out a great many small shapes accurately in card, paper, leather and fabric. For a time he visited a shoe manufacturing firm and used their hydraulic press but this was inconvenient so he approached The Council for Small Industries in Rural Areas – as it was then called. The cost of installing even a small electric press would have been prohibitive and would have required planning permission for three phase electricity supply. CoSIRA's technical department suggested that a simple iron fly press adapted with cutters made to specification would be adequate. They bought, adapted and delivered the press and even painted it blue and clamped it to the floor – and the cost was £180.

The problem with all these schemes is the gap in language and values between those who draft the terms and artists generally. The multitude of benefits for small businesses aim to have a wide catchment and to prevent abuse or double claiming. Artists are used to regarding themselves and being regarded as a calling rather than a business and this may explain the low take-up of these schemes by the profession. It is a 'culture gap'.

Archives

Archives are the record of your work and business and while they may seem irrelevant when you are young, that is the time to start keeping them. Anyone who has ever researched the early work of some disorganised and aged artist, will know the importance of this. You don't know what the future holds, artists perhaps less than most people, so keep records of your work that are good enough to reproduce, ie good slides and photographs and accurately filed reviews etc as well as information about your business, your contacts and clients. Its use to you as time passes will depend on its orderliness so that you can turn things up, and this is simply another administrative skill. It will also constitute the material you can offer to relevant indexes, national or local, of your work (see page 128).

Legal matters

Many of the most frequent and obvious arrangements that are made have a legal basis; buying and selling are legal transactions and we make these all the time. But unfortunately Murphy's Law (if it can go wrong, it will) is more in evidence over legal matters than apparently any other. Solicitors cost money and charge by time unless you qualify for legal aid so you should try to reserve them for emergencies. Perhaps you should choose a solicitor when you set up in business, as you would find a doctor, and hope only to use him or her when things get too bad.

Many problems that you will encounter while running your small business will be easily solved as you become more experienced and matters of contract are examples. But you may need specialist help at some time and it is as well to know a solicitor in case of trouble. The best way to find one is by the recommendation of a colleague in the same line of business as yourself. Alternatively you can write to the Law Society and ask for the names of solicitors in your area who specialise in art-related matters. But as for avoiding legal pitfalls, the best way to do this is to recognise them when you see them. Then you can take evasive action.

Apart from contacting a solicitor privately, there is a tripartite system of advice for legal and related problems. This consists of solicitors who operate the Legal Aid schemes, Law Centres and Citizens Advice Bureaux.

Legal Aid schemes
The Legal Aid schemes in England and Wales help people of small or moderate means to obtain the help of a solicitor. There are different kinds of Legal Aid which cover legal advice and assistance, Civic Legal Aid and Criminal Legal Aid. A helpful leaflet and a booklet explaining how this operates is available from the Legal Aid Head Office (whose address is in Appendix 1). Provision for Scotland and Northern Ireland is also explained.

Law Centres
There are currently over 50 Law Centres in the country and they tend to be situated in urban areas of deprivation where their need is greatest. They depend for their funds entirely on local government and they offer a free service on legal problems regarding housing, welfare rights, immigration, health, employment and education matters. They are staffed by qualified workers and they work closely with advice centres such as the Citizens Advice Bureau and Housing Aid who refer cases to them for specialist attention.

Citizens Advice Bureau
This is really the first port of call for anyone with a problem and they give more general advice and less specialist action. The bureaux are staffed

by volunteers and one of their functions is to differentiate between trivial and more serious problems and advise accordingly. There are several hundred CABs across the country and, while they will refer a client to legal aid or to the Law Centres, they also deal with enquiries regarding local matters, tourism, leisure or holidays. Their service is free and your local bureau will be listed in the telephone directory.

Contracts

A contract is simply an agreement or arrangement that is intended to be binding on both parties. It can be verbal – as an engagement to be married usually is – but the problem with a verbal contract is that it is subject to the fallibility of memory and different interpretation. As Sam Goldwyn said, 'A verbal contract is not worth the paper it is written on.' No one, or not many people, would write down the terms of an engagement unless there were considerable financial or political implications because it is unlikely either party would forget them, but it is perhaps the only form of contract of any importance that can safely be left to memory.

The most frequent contract that we all make is the contract of sale, under the Sale of Goods Act. You see a priced item in a shop: that is the 'invitation to treat' but not an 'offer to sell'; you go to the shopkeeper and offer the money. You cannot insist that the shopkeeper sells the goods at the price marked on them. The acceptance terminates the contract and if the item later falls to bits or fails to operate, that is a different problem and no one could doubt your completed contract of sale.

Most of the contracts that you make in your professional life will not be so simple. The contract which the shopkeeper made with the person who supplied the goods you have just bought would almost certainly have been evidenced in writing so that there was no mistaking what had or had not been agreed.

A contract has two parts, 'offer' and 'acceptance', and must be made between the parties concerned and not by proxy, that is, no one else can 'stand in' for one of the parties unless an agent is appointed. Problems with a contract arise when the terms are disputed; that is why it is better to have it in writing. Contracts should be typewritten to allow no uncertainty of script, and you should keep a copy and file it where you can find it. It is a sad law of business as well as of the jungle that the weakest are attacked first.

A simple case might be that you are invited to an art college to talk about your first two years as a small business. You are invited by phone and you agree but ask for written confirmation. This doesn't arrive so you send a typed letter confirming the date and time and duration and the fee of £60 to be paid gross and 25p per mile for travel by your car.

You enclose either a copy to be signed and returned or a tear-off slip at the bottom and when two days before you are due there has been no 'acceptance', you phone and charmingly suggest that you will not be turning up if there is no reply.

And you don't go if you haven't had a reply in writing because the local authority will deduct tax from your fee and dispute your mileage as certainly as day follows night. But if you have a contract, it will not be worth their while to dispute it and if you receive your fee and expenses two months later (with a bit of luck) and find the sum is not according to contract, you can insist they honour it.

Contract of commission

Suppose that you are commissioned by your regional arts association to do a mural in a hospital, and this could apply to those working in fabrics or ceramics as well as painters and mural sculptors. Perhaps the money is to be paid by several bodies such as the district health authority, Training Agency and the local authority but it is the RAA which is pooling all these different contributions and who is the commissioning agent. Know who your commissioning agent is; there can be only one for one commission but the agent may sit at the top of a pyramid of contributors.

It is usual for you to make a preliminary visit to the site and discuss the requirements in outline free of charge, as would a builder or a plumber. The commissioner will know your work, that is why you are invited, and you will probably be asked to produce detailed drawn and written proposals with a maquette (if suitable). It is usual to receive payment for these, sometimes 10 per cent of the estimated total, but if this commission is a competition and you enter details along with other competitors, it is usually only the winning entry that is purchased. But some sort of payment for invited proposals should be made as that will demonstrate that both parties mean business. But finally, when you have been invited and have agreed to do the work (that is a verbal contract), make sure that you receive a *Contract of Commission*, setting out, for example:

Names of the parties. Who the agreement is between
Description of the work to be made. Its size, location etc
Materials to be used, their quality, durability and type
Schedule. The completion date and how important it is
Payment. Who pays for materials. Who pays for expenses. But the most important part is the fee; it is usual for one-third of the fee to be paid on signing the contract, one-third when the work is half complete and the remainder when the commissioner has approved the finished work. Payment will usually be on presentation of an invoice and the canny

artist will specify how long payment is to take or you can find yourself unpaid for one instalment when you have completed the next phase. *Copyright* is usually retained by the artist.

These clauses relate to all commissioning contracts but to continue our example of a mural on a site, there should also be a clause regarding: *Access to the site*, what hours the artist can work there; the condition and preparation of the site; what services will be offered, whether it will be clean and warm, the availability or otherwise of a secure store to keep materials, a phone, a lavatory, a tea-pot; if needed, will there be ladders, scaffolding, electric points and extension leads?

What can still go wrong
The main thing that can go wrong is that the commissioners do not accept the work when it is finished. There are two reasons for this: either they really don't like it or else they have found they cannot afford it and are trying to get out of paying. Either way, you are protected by your contract if everyone has done his or her homework. But art is an uneasy article to commission because it develops and changes by its very nature. Michelangelo was only meant to do a little bit on that Sistine Chapel ceiling, and what he actually did was breach of contract.

The second thing most likely to go wrong is that in the case of a mural on site, the people who actually work there may hate the idea in general and your work in particular, and the whole thing may have been set up by an enthusiastic art committee on the basis that art is good for everyone. A sensitive regional arts association officer should not let this happen but it can occur and you are the one left feeling bruised.

There are an increasing number of opportunities in the Health Service for murals, artists in residence and other commissions. This is not because the Health Service districts have money to spare, far from it, but as maintenance and redecoration programmes have been cut, some money has been raised from alternative sources to try to maintain some semblance of charm and interest in the otherwise deteriorating hospital environment. For anyone interested in such work, the Arts for Health centre at Manchester Polytechnic is a fund of information and archival material on what has been achieved, where and how.

If you are working on a mural away from home it can be uncomfortable and lonely, and while this does not affect the eventual work of art, it is best to sort out who will find accommodation and pay for it. Also, key people at the site will be the caretakers so ask them what they do and don't want you to do, ie smoking, paint down the sink, lights and security. Their goodwill will make a lot of difference to the care given the work once you have finished. It is amazing how a caretaker who has enjoyed your company can stop trolleys damaging your mural years after you have left.

This mural example pertains to a painter but the principles and problems are valid for any commission. The Crafts Council has produced an excellent leaflet called *Working to Commission* which any craftsperson contemplating a commission would be wise to read. Similarly, for any section of the fine arts profession. *Art Within Reach* (see page 142) is a must for anyone even thinking of a public commission as it discusses matters such as the necessity for planning permission for public works. It also illustrates several of the most exciting recent public commissions and shows just what can be done. (It is now sadly out of print, but it is worth tracking down a copy. There is one in The Arts Council library.)

The laws that govern our lives are complicated, hence the legal profession to interpret them. But in the daily life of a trading artist, this basic understanding of contract is essential and you will be making contracts all the time. The golden rule is 'Get it in writing'. As Mae West said, 'God is love, but get it in writing'.

Equal Opportunities Commission

There has traditionally always been a high proportion of women practising in the different arts and recent surveys have confirmed this but also that they earn proportionally less than their male counterparts. It is therefore appropriate at this stage to refer to the Sex Discrimination Act of 1975 for it can and does have a significant effect on the working lives of women today.

The Sex Discrimination Act applies to Great Britain but not to Northern Ireland and its aim is to make discrimination between men and women unlawful. It applies to education, employment, the provision of goods, facilities and services and the disposal and management of premises.

The Equal Opportunities Commission was set up to help enforce this legislation and to promote equality of opportunity and, if you feel that you have experienced discrimination on grounds of gender, you can write for advice and guidance to the Commission. This applies both to men and women but usually women are more discriminated against.

The Act specifies that women cannot be refused a mortgage, lease, loan, job, insurance, service, purchase or hire or be offered terms that would not be asked of a man, such as a male guarantor on a loan. In job interviews you should not be asked questions that would not apply to your male counterpart, such as how you will organise your domestic affairs. There is also indirect discrimination such as a requirement to be six feet tall or to specify that 'pregnant persons need not apply'.

Generally, cases of discrimination are hard to prove, and you have to have strong evidence but the instances most likely to occur will probably be to do with property and finance, and it behoves women to be aware of their rights on these matters.

The acknowledged discrimination against women on matters of tax is now being reformed under the current Finance Act (see page 32). The Equal Opportunities Commission have published a 'Response' to the Chancellor's 1988 Budget proposals that are the basis of the Finance Act which reviews the changes from the point of view of sexual discrimination. It is clear to read and available from the EOC Offices.

The artist as manager

The act of setting up a business consists first of a private decision to do so. You should then tell your local Tax Inspector and, if you have worked previously, you will need to forward to him your P45 form. You should also tell your local office of the Department of Health and Social Security and arrange how to buy your National Insurance contributions and this is necessary even if you are only working part-time for yourself and still have an employer. These are the only legal requirements unless your anual turnover exceeds £22,100 per annum (1988-89 figure) in which case you must register for VAT (see pages 35–6).

Sole trader

When you work on your own your legal status is that of a sole trader. You are the entire business and there are no legal requirements before you can start. You take all the profit and suffer all the loss. You can employ people if you wish. The disadvantage is that if you fail and cannot pay your creditors, they can claim not only your business assets, such as your equipment, but also your private possessions, such as your house. One way to safeguard your home, if you are married, is to transfer the title to your spouse or to anyone else for that matter, but the situation may be difficult in the event of divorce.

If you decide to trade under a name other than your own, for example if you choose a trade name such as Woody Wonders, then you are bound to disclose your name and address on all correspondence and printed paper, such as invoices. This is required under the Companies Act 1981 whereby you no longer have to register a business's name but you do have to make its ownership clear.

Partnership

A partnership can be made between two or more people who own the business and are equally responsible for its debts, profits and tax affairs.

A partnership does not require any legal documentation – it can exist on a private agreement – but it is recommended that an agreement is drawn up by a solicitor because a vague arrangement that is open to dispute has dissolved many a friendship and even marriage. If a partnership starts and remains an informal arrangement and then a dispute arises, the courts do have standard terms and conditions to apply from the Partnership Act 1890 but it is in no one's interest to let matters deteriorate that far. As with the sole trading situation, you have to tell the Tax Inspector the names of the owners of the business but otherwise it is merely advisable that you draw up the following type of agreement:

1. The partnership's purpose and objectives
2. How much capital is to be contributed by each partner
3. The role of each partner
4. How the profits and losses will be divided
5. How the financial matters will be handled
6. Who will sign the cheques
7. How the partnership can be dissolved
8. How new partners can be appointed
9. A formula to cover the death or prolonged sickness of partner(s)
10. Holidays and hours of work
11. How disputes can be resolved.

The advantages of a partnership are that you share both the responsibilities and the liabilities and you are less isolated than a sole trader. The disadvantages are that if one partner turns renegade, the others can be left with debts. Also, it is seldom that different people have equivalent energy and commitment to a purpose and it is usually the most energetic one who starts to feel aggrieved at carrying an unfair share of the load. For this and for tax reasons it can therefore be an advantage for one person to remain a sole trader and employ those colleagues who might be candidates for partnership, but this will depend on circumstances.

Unincorporated associations
An unincorporated association is recognised as a legal body; the 'unincorporated' means that its members have not registered it as a company limited by guarantee. There are several sorts of groups that come into this category: clubs, societies, co-operatives, institutions or, simply, groups. These groups are formed by people with interests and aims in common who agree to abide by certain rules and procedures. Some artists find that to work in a cooperative suits them well and the Co-operative Development Agency will give you help on joining or setting up. Basically a co-operative is a business owned and controlled by the people who work in it, unlike a partnership which can employ

outsiders. Each person has one vote and the aim is to fulfil the object in hand and any profits are distributed to members only. It can work well for a group of people who have very similar aims and abilities and many studios are run by co-operatives, on a non-profit-making basis.

Limited company

Some artists start their career as a sole trader and then form a partnership and, when the business expands, turn themselves into a limited company.

A limited company is a legal entity that exists independently of its members; it can sue and be sued, have its own bank account, and the shareholders' liability is limited to the value of the shares they hold in it. The personal possessions of the shareholders are therefore not at risk as they are in a partnership or for a sole trader. This is the main advantage of registering yourself as a company.

The disadvantages are that it is expensive and time-consuming to set up and you need the help of your accountant and solicitor; it is a professional's job. A company must have at least two directors. It has to be registered at the Companies Registration Office with details of who is running it and its financial position. The information has to be updated each year and this involves some detailed accounting. Furthermore, if you ask a bank for a loan or a building society for a mortgage, they are likely to ask you (as a director) for some personal guarantee as a surety for their money, and this immediately cancels out the protection the company offers to shareholders. The only slight further advantage of setting up this company is that it gives your operation status, other companies may respect it more, pay debts more quickly and generally act as if they are dealing with a corporate body that they understand rather than a group of lone artists afloat in the world of business.

All artists' circumstances and requirements are different and it may only gradually become clear which sort of organisation your own should be. Start as a sole trader, or as a partnership – they are simple; and then, as you find your feet in the business world, you can decide if you wish to form a co-operative or a company.

Employing staff

If your work and your business develop, you may find that it becomes too much for one person to manage and you decide to buy yourself some help. This could be domestic or administrative help or assistance with your studio work and many craftspeople use 'outworkers' who take work to do in their own homes, such as painting or sewing or assembling. But staff working for you on or off your premises are your employees and you must employ them according to the rules and regulations.

These rules and regulations can be obtained from your local Jobcentre but there is a Freefone for all employment matters which operates from Glasgow. Since this is the only such Freefone for the whole of the UK, it can be difficult to get a reply, but persevere; it is worth it. Phone 0800 393539 between 9.00am and 4.30pm Monday to Friday, and if your query is complex, they are prepared to phone you back with the reply.

Part-time employees

A part-time employee is one who works for you less than 16 hours a week and no contract of employment is needed. But if you pay them more than £41 per week (1988-89) then you will need to contribute to National Insurance and make the necessary deductions, over £50 a week, and you will need to deduct income tax as well. If you employ your spouse, you will still need to make the PAYE deductions if you pay him or her more than the current 'cut-off' figure, but a contract of employment will not be necessary.

Because it is simpler to employ part-time staff and also cheaper because you do not have to pay NI contributions, many employers take on part-time instead of full-time staff. This may be ideal for the employer but the employee remains vulnerable and ill-protected compared with full-time employees' rights. It is usually women who are in this position and this 'second division' of labour is a matter of concern to the TUC and other unions. How this will influence you in your business dealings with employees will be matter for your conscience and circumstances.

Full-time employees

The best place to find out the current regulations regarding full-time employees is the local Citizens Advice Bureau. Alternatively, the DHSS will tell you about the NI contributions due from you and the employee, the Inland Revenue will give you the tax details, and the Health and Safety Officer at the District Council will know about the health and safety regulations. There are also special requirements for employees under the age of 18 and the Race Relations and Sex Discrimination Acts each require that your recruitment and employment should be unbiased. If you employ more than 20 people, you are also required to take on a percentage of disabled people.

This mass of rules is known to deter employers from taking on full-time staff but to ignore them is the best way to land in trouble. Many artists and craftspeople want only one employee and the first requirement is to operate PAYE and make the Class 1 NI payment. The best explanation of this and the other regulations is given in the Department of Employment booklet *Employing people*.

Contract of employment

If someone works for 16 hours a week or more for you, after 13 weeks you will be required to provide a contract of employment that should include: names of the parties involved, rates of pay, and when it is to be paid, hours and conditions of work, holiday pay and entitlement, sick pay, notice from either side and grievance procedures. If someone is doing a specific job for you over a set period, it is as well to have a contract to that effect so he or she cannot claim permanent employment at the end of it. It is also necessary to provide, on each pay day, an itemised pay statement.

Personal welfare, health and insurance

Unless you can afford staff, you will represent your own entire workforce so if you are ill, your business will experience a 100 per cent closure. If you drink too much and eat unwisely, a hangover will not help you and it is better to have one of those casseroles that go on forever than three Mars bars and wonder why you feel dispirited. According to reliable sources, most artists and craftspeople work at least 60 hours a week but if you do have time out of your studio for any reason, it is important to keep the impetus going, either by simply cleaning your tools or clearing up.

Injury or illness is dreaded by all the self-employed but you can insure yourself against this rather than rely solely on sickness benefits. An insurance broker will advise you and again the best way to find one is by personal recommendation but they are also listed in the Yellow Pages or you can write to the British Insurance Brokers' Association and ask for details of those who live in your area. A good broker will be able to suggest schemes suitable for your needs but there is a very comforting system of combining two schemes and these are:

Accident and sickness insurance protects you from the onset of illness for one or two years. This can overlap with permanent health insurance (which should perhaps be called permanent sickness insurance) as it will insure you until retirement or beyond. The point of these two schemes is that the first is designed to pay you throughout a serious but curable illness, such as glandular fever, and the second for an illness that is permanent, such as multiple sclerosis. How much they cost depends on your health, your age and the degree of protection required.

This matter of insurance has considerable financial implications for the self-employed; in other words, sensible cover for all the things you ought to insure is surprisingly expensive.

Apart from health and accident insurance, you will probably be required to insure your life and property if you have a mortgage. If you work for yourself, all your stock and equipment will need to be insured, besides goods in transit and your vehicle. If you undertake public commissions, you may want to take out insurance against public liability (see page 80) and even against legal costs, but all this will depend on the scale of your operation.

Unions and organisations for the self-employed

It has been emphasised that there is no protection for the self-employed on the same level that, for example, NALGO or the NUT protects its members. There are a number of guilds and associations that provide a professional forum for the different arts disciplines but none of them wields legal protection for their members or makes political representation. They fall into different categories and the best known of them are mentioned below. Addresses are given in Appendix 1.

The self-employed can get general help from the National Federation of Self-Employed and Small Businesses who offer access to a private health service scheme and can also help with small commercial mortgages.

Several specialist crafts guilds and societies provide mainly information for members and sometimes help in selling or promoting work. They are listed in the Crafts Council book *Running a Workshop* and Contemporary Applied Arts (formerly the British Crafts Centre) in Covent Garden, London is in touch with the main crafts guilds and associations. The Chartered Society of Designers (once the SIAD) offers advice and information to those working as designers and includes information on standard royalty contracts. The Printmakers Council is one of the best professional bodies and 'aims to promote the position of printmaking as an art form' with exhibitions and publications and, by comparison, the traditional fine artists are a group of determined 'non-joiners'. Art teachers in secondary, higher or further education have the National Society for Education in Art and Design (NSEAD) which is an amalgam of the old SEA and NSAE. This is a trade union as well as a professional association which means that it can make legal representation for its members besides operating schemes such as beneficial insurance policies.

The Artists Union was active in the 1960s and early 70s, but in 1985 the National Artists Association was formed. It now has nine branches across the country and intends to establish others, with a co-ordinator in Sheffield. Its aim is to act as a representative body for artists regarding decisions affecting their economic and working conditions and to engender communication and co-operation between artists. Five weekend conferences are held each year in different parts of the country and all subscribing members receive a bi-monthly *Bulletin* which reports on conferences and information from the branches. Its activities are regularly reported in *Artists Newsletter*.

The business of a small business may seem daunting but, like parenthood, it builds up gradually and you usually have time to learn as you go. It might be advisable to work for a few months in a conventional job before you set up your own business so that you can see what is involved in running a business. It may also make you a better employer when the time comes.

Chapter 5

Premises

Location

Where you decide to live and work will depend on financial, professional and personal factors. It is very unlikely that you will have enough money for the ideal studio early in your career; a studio in Bloomsbury has cost much more since the Bloomsbury Group moved on but whether you rent or buy, and where, will depend on your income, your market and your personality.

Consider your product and its likely market. If you paint huge and unrollable canvases, you should live in a centre for road and rail freight transport; if your work is minute and can rely on a jiffy bag in the post you could live on Skomer or Arran (both have good precedents for the creative life). If you regularly supply goods to an outlet or client, it is often cheapest, in the long run, to live nearby as contacts develop and nothing replaces personal involvement. Also, if you require services such as print, video studios, or are sharing a kiln, these are usually in an urban centre. While your soul may need isolation, to afford it you must also consider customer traffic and practical issues should predominate early in your career.

You may yearn for a country cottage to convert, with a barn to make into a studio and by all means pursue it, but the difficulties will be considerable. The landlord/mortgagee/local planning officer will probably be of conservative country farming stock and wary of any weirdoes, and if you are buying, mortgages are difficult to raise on derelict, out-of-the-way properties, although there are some Rural Development Areas grants (see page 73). It is very expensive to live and work off the beaten track and self-sufficiency is a career in itself. You may be inspired by the smiling fields but the reality may be that the gas cylinder runs out on a wet Sunday, the cabbages are eaten by slugs and the chickens by foxes (ditto cats; a fox will take a dopey cat). As a final note from one who knows, the only real health risk in the country is from rats whose urine can transmit hepatitis: no matter how much rural squalor you can tolerate, beware of rats on your ethnic herb garden.

When you are self-employed, all discipline is self-generated so it is important to live in a manner and a place that suits you. If you are gregarious and need the company of like-minded souls, then it would be best if you joined one of the large urban studio complexes which rent out studio space while rural isolationists can seek their idyll as far as they can afford it.

Is it legal to work at home?

The answer is that it is all a matter of degree. Local authority restrictions were introduced for the best of motives as part of a massive nineteenth- and twentieth-century endeavour to improve public health and well-being by regulating working and living conditions and trying to separate them. Many of these well-intentioned regulations now seem ridiculous when applied to very different modern circumstances but they are still the law whether you obey, bend or evade them.

Most domestic leases, tenancy agreements and mortgages for home owners (besides domestic insurance policies) have a clause requiring the occupier to use the premises for residential purposes only. If either the tenant or the owner is found to be working from home, he or she can be ordered to stop and, if you happen to be preparing for your first significant show or commission, the results can be dire indeed.

As part of the current self-employment trend, there has been a national directive to local authorities to make greater allowance than previously for small businesses in residential areas but it is chance how much notice your local planning officer will take of this. There are two courses of action in these circumstances. One is to work quietly and cleanly, hope for the best and never to advertise your address. The second course (which may not be suitable in all cases) is to write to the mortgagees or the landlord and explain that you wish to carry out your artistic activities at home and they may well be persuaded to agree if you undertake the following:

- Not to trade or sell from home
- Not to install any industrial equipment (ie anything needing three phase electricity)
- Not to cause any disturbance, noise or fumes
- Not to store materials that are a fire or health risk (ie aerosols or solvents) or pollutants (ie dyes down the sink) or disfigure the appearance of the property with piles of stores.

The best course may be to work as usual, say nothing locally and make sure no one has cause to complain. Neighbours who are disgruntled by late night parties may complain about your humble pottery or sculpture studio as a veiled objection to your domestic habits. The nature of your activities will bear some relationship to the trouble you encounter;

graphics, jewellery, illustration and painting are usually quiet, but sculpture, furniture making and any heavy constructional work are bound to be noisy and are perhaps best done elsewhere.

However quiet you may be, you will be contravening Planning Regulations by changing the use of the building by living and working there as opposed to simply living there. Under the present 1971 Planning Act, studios as a category simply do not exist and a designated work-space is either for office or for light industrial use. Local authorities are wary of allowing mixed use of premises because the homeowner may not welcome delivery vans coming and going all day in order to service the 'light industry' next door. The Planning Act defines as 'light industry' any process whereby goods that are to be sold are processed, made or part made. Therefore, all artists and craftspeople fall into this category and, strictly speaking, require planning permission.

But thousands of such people quietly work away and the planning officers would be inundated if every case that should be, was brought before them. Practical general advice can therefore be summarised as follows: until you regard your premises as fairly permanent and provided your activity is self-contained and invisible to neighbours, keep working quietly. If you are bound to be loud and noisy, if you become very famous, or if you settle permanently in the property, then seek informal advice from your planning officer who may be delighted to leave you alone.

If you do buy a property intending to work from it, it can be an advantage to buy somewhere in which some making process has already been established so that you do not change the use of the premises. One small 'light industry' can give way to another with a minimum of hassle.

Let us imagine a painter who has obtained enough regular freelance work to take on the mortgage of a small terraced house which had four basic rooms, two up and two down. She converted the largest, lightest one into her studio with one corner reserved as her office. Both the planning officer and her mortgage company were satisfied with this because she did not overtly trade, she was no nuisance and harboured no danger, she was taxed under Schedule D as self-employed so she claimed one-quarter of the costs of the house as being directly used for her profession; these included mortgage repayments, house insurance, rates and maintenance costs. Under pressure of work, she treated herself to a cleaner and she claimed one-quarter of this cost also (see page 29).

The question of the legality of working from home has already been dealt with but there is one main advantage that in admitting to it, you can claim against Schedule D tax those parts of the premises that are used for your work. Conceal your activities, and you cannot do this. These procedures may seem complicated when all you wish to do is find a room and paint in it but as you produce more work and, hopefully, as you become successful, your most important asset will be your studio and these issues will come into their own in that event.

As a summary of the question 'May I work from home?' the answer is that if you do so from premises where such things have not been done before, you may well be acting unlawfully in common with thousands of others. In practical terms, the answer is that if you cause trouble, you will meet it. Quiet and unobtrusive activities can be carried on for years but even if you make kites out of paper or sculptures out of straw, you are a 'Light Industry' and you had better hope for a planning officer who likes a quiet life and an empty in-tray.

Finding premises

When you have decided in which part of the country you want to live, you can find out if there are any existing group studios in the area by asking your local arts organisations (explained in Chapter 10), your district council or county arts and recreation department. There is a chapter on studios and lists of group studios across the country in *The Artists Directory* (Art Guide Publications) but these tend to be for fine artists and the Crafts Council and the RAAs will know about studios for crafts and applied arts. If you are in London, ACME or SPACE are organisations that exist to help artists find suitable premises. If they all say there are no group premises, it is safe to assume there are none (and there are not many in Great Britain). Then you can either set about founding one or, more simply, you can look for a single studio.

Your most important source of information on available premises will be the local authority, estate agents and the local newspapers; all the papers should be in the local reference library where you can list them and their publication days and make sure they cover the whole of your area. You can look for straightforward advertisements and also (ghoulishly) for bankrupt firms that might well be prepared to let empty premises to artists in order to keep out squatters. If you wish to be really thorough, you could send an advertising postcard with 10p to every post office (they are listed in the telephone book) asking for premises. Ask friends but do not underestimate professional jealousy; if a rabbit finds a good clover patch, it does not waste eating time by going to tell the others. From the time you set up 'in business' you are everyone's competitor and they are yours. Sharing the goodies will be an exception, not an expectation.

You can go out and look for unused property; this is best done by bicycle and you will need a notepad and local map. Unused rooms above betting shops, farm barns and old stores show up by being dark when everything else is lit but all this prowling and searching assumes that you know what you are looking for.

A checklist of requirements could include the following:

- Are you looking for working *and* residential premises?
- What can you afford to pay per square metre?
- What size do you need?
- Does it need to be on the ground floor for access and weight bearing?
- Do you need a strong floor to hold a kiln/press/safe etc?
- Will you need other than the usual facilities (power, heating, WC, water) eg three phase electricity?
- Will you need to soundproof it or put in extra security window bars?
- What can you afford to spend on it (just white paint or a new staircase)? Unless you regard the studio as very permanent, it is best to put your money into items that you can move with you eventually, ie flexishelves rather than 'built to fit'.

These days there are few bargains because landlords are better aware of the value of property so once you have found your ideal but expensive property, you must work out not only whether you can afford to take it on but also to run it.

You can find the rateable value from the rates office but this may be upgraded if and when you apply for planning permission to change its use into 'light industry'.

If you find your property by cycling along in the dark with binoculars, you will then need to find the owner. The corner shop is a source of all local property information or you can write to an owner via the rates office who will forward a letter even if they will not divulge an address.

Example of how not to write a letter to the rates office, (or indeed anyone else)

- Use lined or scruffy paper.
- Handwritten letters are more difficult to read than typed ones and imply that no copy has been kept by the sender.
- No name and address of recipient which means that the letter will probably be handed around until it finds the correct officer.
- No phone number with your address (which is a disadvantage) and no post code.
- Addressed to 'Dear Sir' which is annoying for any woman receiving it; a name is best.
- Content of the letter is unclear in its request and contains irrelevant information.

- Signed off as 'Yours truly' which shows unfamiliarity with letter writing.

Example of a letter likely to get results

- Letter-headed paper (this can be hand done on cheap paper but something should make it visually memorable).
- Well typed and laid out (you are an artist, after all).
- Correctly addressed to the right person (this means they will feel guilty until they have dealt with it; anonymity breeds irresponsibility).
- Clear request for what you want, emphasising the local nature of the enterprise.
- A stamped, self-addressed envelope enclosed shows you mean business and expect a reply. Also, the quality of your address could bear a moment's consideration; if you live in a well-known squat or a communal house recently raided for drugs, it might be wise to borrow a more acceptable address for the purposes of this letter and, if this seems outrageously bourgeois, ask yourself 'what price success?'

Lease or licence

Once your excellent letter has provoked an interested response from the owner of the property, you will need to consider the terms whereby you will occupy it.

A lease or an agreement for a lease/tenancy agreement is a written contract giving certain statutory privileges. A licence is a verbal or written agreement giving very limited right of occupation and, as an illustration of the difference between the two, in the case of a lease the landlord will only have right of entry by reasonable notice to the occupants and so should not have keys but under a licence the landlord has right of entry. Since you will probably invest some time, money and effort in this, it is better if possible to have a lease drawn up to protect your interests as well as those of the landlord and this is normally done by the landlord's solicitor but you will have to bear the costs.

The terms

You will need some money in hand even to consider taking on a studio, so when you make an offer to the landlord, having rejected politely his inflated asking price, make it reasonable and not derisory. Point out the advantages of having reliable tenants in his otherwise empty and vulnerable property and what you will do to improve it. If the premises need a lot of work done to them then don't consider a short tenancy; three to five years should be allowed for any constructional repairs needed, and sometimes rent is waived while repairs are done.

Assess what this studio is going to cost you. If it is in good condition, the rent will be more, if it is in poor shape, it will need more repair, eating into your time and resources. The most important part of any property that you should inspect is the roof.

Capital costs

These will vary from merely the cost of a van to move in to the cost of considerable renovation, for which you will need organisation and a set of good tools (most tools are made for the average sized man not the average sized woman and this is a manufacturing and marketing gap). Usually the landlord is responsible for all outside repairs, such as the roof, and the tenant for inside repairs, such as floors. Costs to the tenant may include:

- Repairs and alterations to ceiling, walls, partitions and floors in accordance with Building Regulations.
- Installation of fire doors and escapes in accordance with the local fire officer's standards.
- Installation of power and heating as necessary, water and services.
- Painting, cleaning and installation of furniture and equipment.
- Purchase of any fixtures and fittings from the landlord or previous tenant and, while it may not look as if there are any, even mouldering light fittings half a mile above your head can come into this category.
- Legal and surveyors' fees; the worse the property, the more these will be.

You will probably need to deal with the planning officer for 'change of use', the Borough Surveyor's department and the building regulations officer for the structural repairs and alterations, and the fire officer. All these officers are at your local district offices and it is best to inform them of your intentions. If you don't need their involvement, they will tell you so.

Running costs

These are the costs of running the studio from the time you sign the lease, not from when it becomes operational.

- Rent (unless there is an exemption during renovation).

- General rates and water and sewage rates (rates are a local tax on the estimated value of property although they may be abolished under the proposed Poll Tax).
- Insurance
  - (a) Building premium
  - (b) Equipment and stock
  - (c) Third party (otherwise known as occupier's liability; that is to cover clients who fall through banisters).
- Services such as a caretaker and rubbish removal.
- Telephone.
- Heat and light.

Since all this represents a considerable outlay in money, time and energy, it is as well to consider the lease and its preparation carefully. The best book on this is the *Artists Studio Handbook* produced by Artic Producers Ltd but it is now a long time out of print so search libraries for it and press for a reprint. For help with the lease you could ask your Citizens Advice Bureau or a local Law Centre if there is one. If you are a craftsperson, you can use the Crafts Council but they will probably direct you to the relevant RAA. ACME and SPACE are both London-based organisations that deal with artists' studios and are described on pages 73–4.

The most usual things to go wrong are that it all costs more than was anticipated and has to be abandoned; that if it is a group of any sort, the most energetic person does most work and gets resentful; the members leave and replacements cannot be found; that the landlord so likes the improvements that the rent is rapidly increased or the area is redeveloped and everything demolished. It might be simpler after all to buy or build a studio.

Buying and building

When you consider in which part of the country you wish to live, you may be guided by the discrepancy in house prices. The inflation in house prices is now so fast (and it is likely to be accelerated by the proposed Poll Tax) that for those on a low income, expediency may overwhelm preference. A mortgage is usually calculated on two and a half times your average salary, and the average may be taken over the last three years, so whether or not to buy will depend on your financial credibility. The advantages of owner-occupation are self-evident, hence its rise in post-war popularity but basically it means that you are unlikely to go bankrupt suddenly because you can always convert your property back into cash and in our inflationary situation, you will (almost) always get more than you paid.

It may be that when you are paying rent, you realise that the same monthly outgoing could be paying a mortgage and that is the time you could well consider purchasing. The most usual sources for a mortgage are the high street banks and the building societies and they all have their own rules and conditions but they are all the same in that they are prompted by business profit, not loss. They will need to be convinced that you have the financial means to make your monthly repayments without default and that you will not decamp leaving them with a troublesome situation. For this reason, they usually insist on life insurance.

Artists are correctly recognised as a profession whose earnings are well below the national average; some make good money and it can be done, but numerically very few, and fewest of all in the 'fine art' league. So this book assumes that its readers are experiencing the usual financial restrictions of the barely established artist or craftsperson; therefore the following suggestions are made for those who cannot afford to buy a separate home and studio but pursue the most usual course of combining them.

Suppose that you buy a typical terraced, semi-detached or detached house; consider what opportunities there are for a studio, having first identified your studio requirements. Do you need height and access, light, a strong floor, warmth, sound-proofing, security, all of these? Look at the loft, and if you decide that it has a future, you could consult the Loft Shop in Croydon who have done for lofts what the Sock Shop has done for socks. Alternatively, look at the outbuildings and also at the house surround: is there any area that could be simply roofed? Older properties in run-down areas can be the most promising because they often have a plethora of pigsties and run-down privies. If you are going to need three phase electricity for a kiln or other equipment, to be on the route of an electric cable carrying this can save thousands of pounds if circumstances are right.

Some country properties are cheaper if they are surrounded by a mass of old-fashioned rights of way, pathways and patches of land of which the ownership is unclear. What you gain from such a purchase in cheapness you may lose if you want to extend or convert. In such a case, you should check your deeds very carefully or even get a solicitor local to the area to check them for you as it will be laid down somehow what you can and can't do. Alternatively, you can consult the Land Registry at your county offices. This was started in 1928 as the compulsory registration of property and 90 per cent of the country is now covered. It is accessible

71

to anyone anxious to know whether they own the path, pigsty or well, or where, within that sea of stinging nettles, their boundary actually lies.

Having found a suitable property, building a studio is not as expensive as you may think. Take the case of a fabric designer who bought a small terraced house and needed a studio. On the back of her house, she had a redundant lean-to privy, and she owned the party wall which was 12 feet away. The architect she approached quoted £10,000 for her envisaged room. This might as well have been ten million so she thought again.

This is an actual example and the costs are those applying in 1983-84. She approached the Building Centre in London who stock a mass of information about building products and guidance on building problems for those undertaking their own design and building. The Royal Institute of British Architects have a Clients Advisory Service to help people design their own buildings in accordance with current regulations which, if you are able to tackle it at all, is the way to avoid an architect's fees. To apply for this service you have to measure and photograph the area which in this case was 12 x 25 feet, and specify what you want. Once the designs were roughly worked out, the heroine of this story asked the RDC to draw them to the satisfaction of the local authority building inspector. The consultancy cost £20 (which at that time was with the Building Centre whose service is now discontinued) and the RDC drawings £150, and there was also a building inspection fee of £40. Building Regulations are operated by the district council and they are an obligatory standard aimed at making sure that all building is safe and alterations accord with health regulations. She found a local builder and, once he had built the fairly simple structure, she did some of the plastering and all the painting and the total cost was £4,600. She paid for it by extending her mortgage, as the bank had a policy of helping small businesses; the rates increased, as did the heating costs and the house insurance, but because the value of the property was enhanced, it was felt to be worth it and the value still came within the limit for Capital Gains Tax on resale (see page 34).

The position regarding planning permission was as follows. As a fabric designer working at home, she had applied for planning permission but the officer said that since she was quiet and did not advertise as a selling outlet, she did not need it. Her equipment was no different essentially from domestic applicances, she needed no extra electricity and she checked with the water board that the amount of dye she discharged was at an acceptable level. But on building the studio, the second requirement for planning permission arose. You need planning permission to change the use of a place, to alter it in certain ways, or extend it. The extension must be under 70 cubic metres or more than 15 per cent of cubic capacity of the existing building (whichever is less) and the start of this sum is to work out the cubic capacity of the original building including the roof space, the chimneys and the lean-to privy you intend to demolish. If your extension is bigger than 15 per cent of the total or over 70 cubic metres, you need permission; if it is smaller, you do not. On this occasion, the studio extension was just small enough not to qualify. Result, no planning application had to be made.

This was a financial undertaking on a small and irregular salary that was perfectly possible and the benefits to her work and the increase in her capital assets justified the outlay.

Improvements grants

Home improvement grants may still be available from some district councils for the renovation of domestic property but their availability has always varied across the country and they have been affected by severe economies. In the Rural Development Areas there are still grants available for the conversion of redundant buildings into workshops and again, while these vary across the country, the situation can be checked with the local branch of the RDC.

Specialist organisations

Two organisations that have considerable experience of locating, leasing and converting property in which artists can then live and work are SPACE and ACME. They are both London based and deal only with property within the London boroughs but they advise artists all over the country on studio negotiations.

Air and Space (Arts Services Grants Ltd) consists of the Air Gallery in Rosebery Avenue, London and SPACE studios. SPACE were founded in 1968 to help artists find cheap and adequate studios in London. They do this by licensing to artists studios that they themselves have leased and also by giving information to those outside London on how to find and set up studios in otherwise unwanted property.

SPACE negotiate the lease of the property with the owner who is often but not always the local authority. The property may be unwanted, in need of substantial repair and due for eventual demolition. SPACE then usually negotiate a conversion grant from the Arts Council and arrange for the basic conversion work to be done. Further and final conversion work is done by the artists and their licence is with SPACE, not the owner. Rent is matched to what artists can, on average, afford and although these studios are on a limited lease, this is usually longer than originally anticipated.

SPACE deal only in studios, not living accommodation, but ACME deal with both houses and studios for artists. First founded in 1972 and working on similar principles to SPACE, ACME acquire the leases and organise the conversion of property into studios that are then let to artists. The houses may have a comparatively short life expectancy but are worthwhile restoring for homes and studios.

SPACE and ACME are both charities and therefore claim 50 per cent rate relief which benefit makes these property dealings viable. They are similar in that they both act as agents for artists by finding, leasing, restoring and managing properties for homes and studios, so saving individual artists from the hassle of dealing with all the relevant authorities. They both offer property only to fine artists, that is painters, sculptors, print-makers or related activities such as video and independent film-making and not to craftspeople or designers, who should ask the Crafts Council or their RAA for information about any studios for which they could apply.

Most working necessities can be tackled with help from both the specialist agencies such as, in this case, SPACE, ACME and the RAAs, and with those authorities and organisations that exist for all citizens such as the local authorities, the RDC or estate agents. Sometimes it is a combination of their advice and help that can finally solve your particular problem.

Chapter 6

The Product

This chapter is concerned with the objects that you make, your 'product': how to protect it, not from thieves or corruption, but from unlawful use by others. We then discuss product liability and your responsibility for safe procedures and storage, and finally the adaptation of your product in the light of market trends and new technology.

Copyright

This is the protection of writers, artists, composers or other creators of original, artistic work. You do not have to register copyright because it automatically exists once you have completed your original, artistic work, and you cannot copy an idea or an intention, only an object. Copyright is intended to prevent other people copying work to the extent that it could reasonably be mistaken for the original or reproducing pictures of it.

The law relating to copyright is set out in the Copyright Act of 1956 which tells you what is protected. The Act protects original works of artistic craftsmanship that fall into the following two categories:

Group I includes those items one usually thinks of as 'art', that is paintings, sculptures, (including moulds), most sorts of prints, drawings and photographs; all irrespective of artistic merit.

Group II includes all those items which do not fall into this fine art, traditional grouping but which have 'artistic merit'. This does not refer to their qualities as we would understand them but asks whether a work has been created by the originator applying 'skill and taste' to its production with the 'intention of creating an article which would appeal to the aesthetic taste of those who see it'. Thus all the creative crafts fall into this category and also recent developments such as holograms, laser and light works, videos, body art and bookworks. Collages of found objects would be protected, but not the objects themselves until they had been assembled in a 'work of artistic craftsmanship'. Fine crafts would be similarly protected until the point where objects could not be differentiated, such as the mass production of flower pots, when their protection would be by registered design or trade mark.

Work that is original

The legal requirement of originality is that the work must not be physically copied from another work so forgeries are not protected by copyright nor photographs of photographs.

Originators of the work

The final legal requirement concerns the makers of the work. Most people qualify for copyright protection provided they come from one of the countries that signed either the Berne Convention or the Universal Copyright Convention.

How long does copyright last?

It normally lasts during the life of the creators and for 50 years after their death. Thus the copyright for *Wind in the Willows* lasted for 50 years from the death of Kenneth Grahame. Just before this anniversary date, the publishers reissued the book with new illustrations (indeed there were several newly illustrated editions) each of which was protected in its typography and arrangement for a further 25 years. This was to give the publisher some control over its treatment.

There are variations on this 'life plus fifty years' rule regarding photographs, most sorts of prints, joint works and works done under the auspices of the Crown or government departments. No one suggests that copyright is simple and there is furthermore a discrepancy between those countries that signed the Berne Convention on copyright (to which Britain is a signatory) or the Univeral Copyright Convention which offers protection for only 25 years after the death of the originator. The USSR is one of the main signatories of the latter convention.

Who owns copyright?

The general rule is that the first owner of the copyright of any work is the creator of that work, unless the creator is in employment and uses his or her employer's time, facilities and materials to make the work, for then the employer owns it. But the self-employed artist owns his or her own copyright, unless it is a portrait painted on commission.

A work has two facets: the tangible work itself and the intangible copyright, and you can sell both. If you sell a work, you do not also automatically sell the copyright. Usually the sale of copyright is not specified in a sale of work because too often a work is sold by the transfer of greasy fivers to the back pocket, by which action you lose out on your tax deductible expenses, diminish your status as a professional artist and also leave your copyright unspecified with all the implications of future trouble. Refer to Chapter 7 and the contract of sale; the copyright is specified either for sale or retention. If you do not specify (and most artists don't) then all things being equal, the copyright is retained by the originator, except in cases of portraits, engravings and photographs that have been commissioned.

You also have the option of selling limited copyright even when you don't sell the original and this is especially likely in the case of illustrators. (The Association of Illustrators has published guidelines that describe this fully.) Suppose someone sees a piece of your work while it is your possession and wants to use it for reproduction purposes. You can then sell the reproduction rights for that specific purpose and, if those rights are extended without your agreement, that is contravening your copyright.

An example of this refers to an engraver who had work in a gallery when a request was received from a credit card company to use the image in a new advertising campaign. The gallery acted as the artist's agent and negotiated the reproduction rights for a specific purpose, for a specific number of prints and over a specific time. The gallery received commission on the deal, and the artist benefited while retaining possession of the work and with the option to renegotiate further use of the image in future.

Furthermore an artist can sell a work and also sell limited copyright. A painting in one of the national arts council collections was requested for use on a record cover; the arts council negotiated rights for this one use again with specific limitations, the artist getting the fees and the arts council retaining ownership.

One further reason to understand copyright is that while you may own the copyright on a work, you may not be allowed access by the owner to photograph the work to exploit that copyright. This is all the more reason to specify on your sale of contract what it is that you are selling.

But it remains a general public belief that the owner of the work owns the copyright. If someone wants to take a photograph of a piece of work, they would probably ask the owner of the work and never dream of asking the copyright owner, usually the artist. And if they realised they had to do so, they would probably go off and find something less complicated to photograph.

How to sell a copyright

In order to sell a copyright you have to make a written, signed statement to that effect. What you should charge for copyright is even more difficult to assess than deciding what you should charge for your work since you cannot foresee its popularity. J R R Tolkien persuaded a reluctant publisher to accept *The Hobbit* by agreeing to forgo all royalties after sales of a certain number. Agreements of such mammoth miscalculation are now known as 'Hobbit arrangements'.

Copyright is a complicated subject and in the context of this book, not all its ramifications can be discussed. The excellent *Visual Artists' Copyright Handbook* by Henry Lydiate is both clear and detailed (available from DACS – page 140), but the general advice is that you sell limited copyright and this will show that you are aware of the situation and yet will allow your work to be used for those publicity purposes that all artists hope will occur. If use of your work exceeds your permission, you then have clear redress – and this does happen – and dues from infringement of copyright can bring in a sudden rush of money from work long sold and forgotten.

This agreement to limited use will depend on circumstances but you could say that you are willing for any photograph or reproduction to be published of your work provided it acknowledges you and is for publicity and not commercial purposes. Also, you can specify a length of time after which copyright has to be renegotiated because you do not know what the future holds and one day your work may go on a postage stamp and then you would be very sorry that you sold the copyright!

The only exception that should be mentioned here is work in public places of which, due to the united efforts of the RAAs and the Arts Council, there is an increasing amount around. If your work is in a position that is open to the public, your copyright (if you own it) is not infringed in the usual way by taking a photograph or making a film, a TV programme, drawing or engraving of it. It is public property and the price you receive for making it should reflect this.

The copyright sign © is internationally recognised but your work is protected whether you use it or not. The importance of using it is that it shows the matter has received attention; the copyright owner's name is placed alongside with the date of production, as on page 4 of this book.

Design and Artists Copyright Society Ltd (DACS)

You may well feel that you have better things to do than permanently scan the papers and periodicals to see if your copyright is being infringed and so to offer this service of care, an organisation known conveniently as DACS has been set up.

DACS acts for its members who pay a lifetime subscription of £15 plus VAT. It was initially funded by the ubiquitous Gulbenkian Foundation but it now runs on its subscriptions and a percentage of the copyright fees that it retrieves as it is a non-profit making company. It exists to police the unauthorised use of reproduction but its main function is to act as an agent for negotiations of copyright between artists and designers and those with whom they deal, such as publishers, broadcasters etc.

Although it was only founded in 1984 and its publicity speaks clearly to those artists and designers who are new to the game, it has a huge clientele through collaboration with similar organisations in other countries representing their members as they represent ours across national boundaries. Therefore illicit reproductions of Picasso here or Moore abroad will be subject to the same international copyright rules. Since it only acts for clients on matters that arise after membership is taken out, it is as well to join before trouble looms.

Registered designs

The anomalies and inconsistencies of the Copyright Act reflect that it was passed as long ago as 1956 and since then there have been considerable changes in work procedures and reproduction methods. There is a new Copyright Bill at present before Parliament that, in its draft form, substantially revises the Copyright Act. It is complex because it has some years' development to incorporate and it is also designed to predict the future and its needs. All artists would be advised to be aware of its enactment.

Copyright exists automatically on all works of original artistic craftsmanship and it is usual for these items to be limited in number by their nature even if they are produced as an edition. While designed objects that are intended to be manufactured in quantity by some industrial process have the usual copyright protection, they can be given extra protection by being registered as a design.

To register a design you have to apply to the Design Registry which is a part of the Patent Office and you pay a fee on a sliding scale for the protection which lasts initially for five years. The system exists to offer further protection than that given by copyright to designed articles intended for manufacture. 'Designed' means the outward appearance of the item and an 'article' in this context means something that is produced by a manufacturing process in quantity, and that is not hand made. The 'designed article' must also be sufficiently different from all other designed articles and represent a real development, not just an extension of someone else's idea. But the *raison d'être* of a design presented for registration must be its appearance and its function must depend on its appearance.

Lego is a registered design, and Meccano (for those readers old enough to remember it). The plastic popper beads that swept the 1950s teenage 'accessories' market would have been a registered design. Beads are as old as civilisation and various forms of plastic have been around since the 1890s (with patents to protect them), but the design of interlocking cast plastic beads that could be interspersed with each other, made into different lengths and which would 'pop' apart if someone tried to strangle you with them, represent all the qualities required for a 'registered design'.

The Design Registry produces two booklets, *Introducing Design Registration* and *Applying to Register a Design*. The procedures of registration are clearly described, but the candidates for such protection are offered less explanation. However, it links registration with copyright and describes their overlapping, so those in doubt should send for them. They are free.

Patents

A patent is also a form of protection, not for products distinguished by visual exclusivity but for products made or functioning by processes that are the result of invention or discovery. The early synthetic plastics were patented; for example, *bois durci* was an early imitation of jet and the process of making it was patented. Those who then paid a patent fee could use the process to make hundreds of pieces of jewellery according to designs that were, of course, protected by copyright.

Trade marks

Trade marks are a form of protection for a maker who, by stamping, sewing, printing or engraving a distinguished mark of some sort, shows who is the manufacturer. This mark can be a signature such as the red 'Kelloggs', or a symbol, but one of the best known is the Marks and Spencer calligraphic 'St Michael' which is on their millions of items.

Trade marks have to be registered at the Patent Office where you can also check to make sure that a trade mark you would like to adopt does not coincide with an existing mark. Trade marks carry over 40 different classes of use but the Patent Office will advise you.

Liability for your product

The extent to which you are responsible for the safety of your product comes under the umbrella term 'product liability' as it pertains to any manufacturer. You are bound to take normal precautions regarding the safety of your product for the protection of those who handle or own it. For example, if you make toys and they constitute an unreasonable hazard to children or if your sculpture requires electrical installation and it is not earthed and wired according to regulations, and your product injures someone, you could be sued for negligence.

If you have any reason to be especially wary of such possible reprisals, then you could ask your insurance broker (see page 60) about possible insurance against such claims. Such policies are much more usual in the USA but it can be a wise precaution wherever you live.

If your work is shown in a public situation, once it is accepted and purchased its safety is normally a matter for the owners. For example, if after five years a mural sculpture that you made falls off the wall because the brackets have rusted, then that is the responsibility of the owner as it would be for a car that rusted after five years, but if pieces fall off because you have not used the correct materials, the public and the owners may have a case against you. This is another part of the 'contract of commission' (see pages 53–5) that could bear consideration.

Safety in manufacturing processes

The Building Regulations officer and the planning officer will between them make sure that your newly built or converted studio will not fall down and kill you, nor that your health will succumb by the cesspit being too shallow or the lavatory being next door to the kitchen. Until or unless you employ people or you invite people regularly to your premises, you will be responsible to yourself only, except that you are required as a member of society to take 'reasonable care'.

There is an excellent book produced by Tim Challis and Gary Roberts called *A Guide to Safe Practice in the Arts and Crafts* which assesses the dangers in the materials that are commonly used in crafts and art practices. Aerosols can explode if you puncture the tin, several adhesives and solvents are dangerous if inhaled, many pigments in paint and ink are poisonous, besides the obvious hazard of lead based glazes. Toxic substances should not be poured down the sink; if you have only a little, dig a hole, and if a lot, telephone your environmental health officer at the district council. Only human debris should go down the lavatory, toxic or not.

Advice given in *A Guide to Safe Practice* is never to use the kitchen for your work but if that advice were to be followed, countless artists would stop production. Toxic substances can stain a draining board, worktops and clothes, so it is less drastic but perhaps more practical to suggest that if you use other than the most innocuous substances in the kitchen, use separate bowls, clothes and containers. Both yourself, pets and children will be at risk not only from a headache that afternoon but ultimately from cancer caused by carcinogenic agents such as several wood dusts and certain pigments. While most artists have to start off using their living quarters as their work space, once you can afford a separate space, keep all materials there and wear a good boiler suit on which the spots

81

and stains will probably gradually become holes, causing you to consider what those agents would do to your inside.

These are the less obvious hazards and it is assumed that equipment such as power tools and kilns will be supervised. Cats will get into a warm kiln and there are horror stories in the potteries of tramps who have crawled into industrial kilns for the warmth and been quietly incinerated; legends from China tell that the finest pottery was always fired with a sacrificed slave.

Insurance

Care of your work while in your home or studio raises some problems. It can be difficult to insure unsold work because of the uncertainty of establishing its price and so a lot of artists insure everything else rather generously and leave the 'stock in hand' uninsured (unless it is valuable jewellery). But there are hazards even in the home and these can be minimised by how and where you store work. Water is a hazard so do not store your work under the water tank or near flammable materials. Shelves can crash down, and light, damp and dust are all damaging agents. If you handle precious materials, never allow these to be seen through the windows and if you need a small safe, there is one called Plugsafe produced by Innovations (PO Box TR1, Lowfields Way, Leeds LS12 6HN) that is disguised as a twin electric socket. If you work from home, any damage or burglary is doubly unfortunate so invest in some form of security. The crime prevention officer at your local police station will advise you but security locks and a dog are the best insurance and both should last you years, unless of course the dog licks poisonous pigment off its feet or inhales the Cow gum.

If you wish to be really thorough, it is a good idea to maintain an inventory of all your equipment and materials with their current valuations against them for insurance purposes. Valuable or unique items can be supported on such an inventory with a Polaroid photograph which could simplify any future claim. Do not lend or borrow items without discussing possible damage and valuation and this applies especially to power tools and vehicles.

Market trends

The idea of simplifying or speeding up your work, aligning it to a new public or deliberately looking for a market gap will be irrelevant to those who are already committed to their work and could not tolerate its disruption. But circumstances can work in an artist's favour as many historic examples show; witness Daumier who had to work in black and white and at speed because his sight was poor and his newspaper demanded quick and monochrome work.

The economic recession has not destroyed the purchasing power of the buying public but it has altered its buying habits, and these have been identified by those in the habit of selling. Have a look at any successful marketing of non-essential goods such as the plethora of shops and stalls at Covent Garden which are characterised by a variety of goods and a range of prices but a uniform standard of merchandise; qualities of attractiveness, invention and uniqueness are also important to 'persuade' purchase. The public are still buying but are paying less on average for each item.

Purchasing habits and basic marketing techniques are applicable to all business but visual fashion is important in this context as nowhere else. Artists can influence, lead or reflect this and one example is a small manufacturing company that designs and makes a range of small household items but mainly clocks. They are all made from wood and painted so as to suggest the sophistication of old-fashioned toy makers and the quirky humour of folk art and cartoons. There has been a tradition of this sort of work since Sam Smith started to produce his 'adult' toys, 'adult' in the sense of 'adults only' films. The firm have capitalised on this market; they have streamlined manufacture, set the prices to catch the market and distributed in quantity all over the country and now enjoy considerable success.

Technical development

In 1972 the Ritchie Report *The Employment of Art College Leavers* suggested that in future art students would be well advised to familiarise themselves with technological opportunities and business understanding if they were to make a living during the second half of the twentieth century.

The spin-offs from technological wizardry that offer visual opportunity are gathering pace but it often seems to be those who are inspired by technical rather than aesthetic adventure who use them. Witness the comparatively staid use in this country of holograms which are still regarded in the art world as clever toys. This may be due to the expense involved, and a series of study opportunities offered a few years ago by the Gulbenkian Foundation aimed to help remedy this.

Craftspeople have more often understood this connection, especially jewellers with their use of anodising and bulk manipulation of acrylics and foil, and modern studio potters have worked with firms such as Wedgwood on new designs. But the firms specialising in, for example, the restoration of tiles and terra-cotta for historic houses by the use of amazing innovative procedures may as well be in a different country from the hundreds of ceramics graduates who pour out of college every year or teachers who find that their career has been curtailed and so become freelance.

The difficulties and expense of acquiring new techniques of any sophistication have been discussed in Chapter 4. Apart from the Gulbenkian Foundation, which ran the Craft Initiative forums during 1987-89, or the RDC, you are unlikely to get any help or advice of this nature from the subsidy bodies because it is simply not within their field. Such advice as there is will probably come from government, employment or academic/technical bodies.

But there are cheaper and more ordinary ways to make this sort of exploration, for example in the rapid expansion of reproductive and printing methods. Do not underrate photocopiers. Ten years ago they could only copy on to their own odoriferous paper, now they are able to copy on to any paper or card, and cheap accurate colour prints on both sides of paper will be the next advance. If you wish to reproduce a monochrome image several times, rather than printing it you could photocopy and then hand colour it. Photocopied images used to be unstable, that is they were expected to fade. They are now said to be 'stable' in so far as anything on paper is so and even a Persil packet would fade eventually. The facility of cheap and good reproduction has made the pirating of work easier which is why it is necessary to be aware of your copyright position and even pay DACS to look after it for you.

This and other inventive means of printing are described by Tony Parkin in his book *Art of Survival*. He has understood very clearly and described in some detail how an artist can reduce costs and present a lot of items in quantity, so that a lot of sales can be made. For example, prints can be taken off perspex or acrylic sheet or vinyl tiles, it doesn't have to be copper or zinc sheet. The old fashioned mangle used to be the poor artist's answer to printing; although it tends to distort any rubbery material, it may be coming back into its own again just as the old Albion presses are becoming valued as collectors' items.

Producing a lot of inexpensive items and selling at a profit is one approach to running a profitable business but the whole gamut of marketing techniques that you can see in any supermarket can be of use. The prints produced for Christmas 1985 for the Band Aid Fund, Art Aid, were in effect a special offer and special offers usually make enough profit for another one to follow.

Chapter 7

Marketing and Selling

Art is not a standard product and all the well-meaning marketing procedures in the world will not necessarily succeed in selling it. Its function is usually obscure, its appreciation often delayed and its production seldom required. Small wonder that so much of it remains unsold. Its relationship to society is clear only after a passage of time and if it does create a need, it may be a need that only gradually becomes apparent.

Obviously this gloomy picture does not apply to functional crafts whose position is obvious, appreciation immediate and production encouraged, and they are no less valuable for this happy state of affairs. Gloom does not equal merit.

Only a small proportion of the art made gets sold, and while this may not matter at a time of national affluence, in a time of national scarcity, it seems to. Either there is too much of it, or of the wrong sort, or the marketing is inadequate, or society doesn't know what's good for it!

Marketing includes setting the scene for selling and this means not only advertising and packaging but also you yourself and how you look and conduct yourself.

Presenting yourself

If this seems outrageous to the free spirit, ask yourself what price a living? You can make a virtue of eccentricity, wild glamour or even squalor but to be late, rude or offensive will not work in your favour. An Afghan coat that smells too like an Afghan goat or wearing swastika earrings could ruin your chances with potential buyers. This is not necessarily urging you to conform to society but just pointing out that if you want its money, don't upset it. Decide on your style and then perfect it and try to mute any too obvious sexual or political opinion or proclivity, for the moment. On the other hand, one of the country's most eminent jewellers was once followed into his London gallery by the police because he looked so awful but he had had the foresight to become the whizz-kid of his art first.

Presenting your product

The 'total packet' approach to your work depends on what you make. (This is the marketing concept that everything you need is in one purchased packet, ie the cod *and* the butter). Any work will look better clean and displayed than not; jewellery gleaming in boxes looks more like jewellery than when muddled up under papers. Presentability and suitable packaging on hand can tip a dithering buyer over into purchase.

It is very persuasive also to be able to give advice on an item's care: tapestries and any textile work should not be wrapped in polythene because dust clings to it – a clean calico bag is best with a firm rod from which to hang it, and its care need only be that given by a clean hoover brush; anodised jewellery loses its anodising so don't scratch it; acid-free tissue paper may be best for your prints but the stuff all looks the same; ammonia brings gold up nicely but silver-dip ruins resin; direct light and heat damage works on paper and some books but what about oil and acrylic? If this collage falls to pieces, don't repair it with any rubber-based adhesives as they discolour after 20 years, put it under perspex but that needs a non-static polish.

If your work is produced as an edition, whether a cast or a print, it is a legal requirement that this is declared and that you give details of the edition. You can make this an opportunity to explain the difference between a reproduction, an original and a print, between a carving and a cast, or between a pot that is salt-glazed, porcelain or raku. Be very patient and educate your public because eventually it will be in your interest to do so.

One part of your selling package is bound to be black and white photographs and colour slides. Is it self-evident to suggest that these should be good ones, taken in focus and with the right sort of lens, each one labelled with the artist's name, title, medium, size and date? Some indication of size can be useful: one jeweller put a 2p piece in each picture and a sculptor included a Coca-Cola bottle beside each piece to indicate its size, but this would mean that the photographs could not be used in any publication.

Use your expertise

There is one particular service that artists can proffer to their public on occasions that redresses the balance of attention now given to 'antiques' and the comparative neglect of twentieth-century artefacts. Television has alerted people to what may be in the attic but less so to what may be in Aunt Annie's flapper days' costume jewellery box or great Uncle Geoffrey's RCA folder. As you meet and deal with clients, keep alert, as your perhaps unusual knowledge could make you trusted and sought for identification or valuation of items. A jeweller was once approached by a client asking her to melt down a gold bracelet to make something new. It was a Tiffany art deco bracelet that sold for many times the melt-down value and the client was completely unaware of its value because it was out of fashion. There are not so many experts for the twentieth century as there are for the eighteenth. It's a market gap which you can fill.

Selling

Art is not a commonplace product (see Chapter 8), and it needs rather special selling. Your reputation as an artist is based on your work and if it is not presented so as to do you credit, you lose credit. Suppose you sell a painting and subsequently find that it has been reframed and, in doing so, part of the original is folded or cut off, do you have any redress? Some local authority art collections are especially bad about this as they reframe paintings to conform to a standard size. If your work is damaged by light or damp, or you find that your work has been damaged and badly repaired, what can you do? A contract of sale can protect the work to a certain extent.

Contract of sale

Henry Lydiate has dealt with this with his customary thoroughness in 'Selling Work' published in *Art Monthly* and one of the *Collected Artlaw Articles* (now out of print but worth seeking in libraries). He has drawn up a contract of sale that is exemplary for items loosely termed 'fine art' or borderline with fine crafts. The only problem is that if you want to sell work, you want to make it easy, not difficult, and to get a purchaser to agree to so many terms might require Henry Lydiate himself there in person to persuade them, as no doubt he would. But the points raised are all to do with the sort of complaints that artists make over the years and particularly towards the end of their careers when they find how their work has been treated.

Basic details

- Date of sale
- Place of sale
- Title of work
- Description: what it is, medium, size etc
- Edition number (if it is an edition)
- Copyright (sold or retained)
- Name and address of purchaser

- Name and address of artist
- Price and method of payment (VAT).

But there are other considerations for both the artist and buyer ideally to undertake.

Artist's obligations

- That the work is the artist's original work and he or she will not produce a replica.
- If the work is one of an edition, that the edition will not be extended.
- Although the artist retains copyright, the owner may allow the work to be photographed for use in magazines etc, if not for the owner's gain (that is, there may be an article about the owner's home and a photograph could include the work; this does happen).

Buyer's obligations

- The buyer undertakes to give the work normal care and not alter it.
- If the work is damaged, the buyer will notify the artist and give him or her the option of repairing or supervising repair of the work.
- If the work is resold, the buyer will inform the artist.
- The buyer will allow the artist to borrow the work back with reasonable notice for exhibition purposes and will allow the artist access for photography. (It can happen that while an artist retains copyright, he does not have the right of access to exploit it.)

The 'basic details' should perhaps be used for any sale of original art or craftsmanship and you could make out a receipt book accordingly. Many artists deplore that they did not keep better track of their work and it can be very difficult to track it down later. As to how many of the artists' and buyers' obligations to impose, this will depend on what you sell; they are hardly suitable for items produced in quantity but any sort of one-off that you value could be considered for such protection.

Resale royalties

The right to claim resale royalties does not yet exist in this country but several clever young agitators are working on it. Basically it is the principle that when a work of art is resold, a proportion of the profit should be paid to the artist who made it. This profit could derive from inflation or from an increase in the value of the piece, either way it would be profit, but if the work is sold at a loss, no one would benefit. It is intended that it would operate only during the artist's lifetime.

France, Germany and Italy are among the European countries that have laws relating to this but California's Resale Royalties Act can stand as a good example of its form and purpose. It enables visual artists to benefit from the continuing economic value of their work in the same way that the Public Lending Right benefits authors and the Performing Rights Society pays composers royalties on the publishing and performing of their music. Artists at present have no benefit from their work once it is sold except for any payments from copyright (providing they have retained it).

The Californian Resale Royalties Act protects the work of the residents of California wherever the resale may be made, even outside America. In order to pay artists what is owing to them, there is a computer register of artists and they have to join this if they want to benefit. The resale profit payable is 5 per cent of the gross price; it does not apply to work selling for less than $1000, nor to works resold for less than the original price or sold after the artist's death.

The benefits to artists of this system are obvious but the fringe benefits are also important. There is no central register of artists in this country. Several attempts have been made to set one up but they have always been discontinued through lack of funds. Most of the RAAs run registers of artists in their regions and craftspeople are well served by a selective Index and a National Register run by experienced staff at the Crafts Council in London.

Artists' agents

It is almost a professional requirement for actors and actresses to use an agent to find work and similarly, many writers rely on a literary agent to find publishers for them. Only artists in the highest tax brackets have a similar system but galleries can agree to act as agents in a limited way for artists that they represent.

In this context, galleries can lay down conditions that, once accepted, must be honoured. These can include an undertaking for exclusive exhibition of your work with that gallery, or a right to all new work, or an agreement not to exhibit within 50 miles or so, or to vary your prices, or evade the gallery's commission on sales in any way. Occasionally a gallery gives an annual stipend to an artist in return for such an agreement and, most usefully, a gallery can act as your agent for the foreign exhibition and export of your work. See Chapter 8 for more information on galleries.

Selling abroad

If a gallery wishes to represent you abroad, it could be assumed that they know what they are doing but you could quietly find out who else has been represented by them and ask if all went smoothly. If you decide to undertake this by yourself, it is as well to have some successful experience of selling your work in this country first. Also, it is advisable to have some reason for sending your work to the particular destination, and initially to concentrate on one place in one country.

Customs and shipping procedures have their rules and regulations and your transactions will be much easier if you understand and conform to them. There is a Small Firms Service booklet on general exporting procedures and the Crafts Council book *Running a Workshop* deals with the export of craft items, while the Artlaw articles in *Art Monthly* have discussed the import and export of fine art. For general enquiries, you could first contact your local Customs and Excise office.

Publicity

This is a broad subject to tackle so we shall subdivide it into radio and television, the national press, the local press, the specialist press and periodicals. The best and most complete press guide is *Willing's Press Guide* which is an annual publication and will tell you more than you could possibly need to know.

Radio and television

You can regard radio as the light cavalry and television as the heavy guns in an army; the light cavalry will be appropriate for an effective, lightning strike but the heavy guns will have to select their target carefully and they need time for manoeuvre.

Whether you are considering independent radio and television or the BBC, it is the regional and local stations that you should approach. If you are handling your own publicity for an exhibition, demonstration, open studio or some other event, then you can send information to the arts or current affairs department of your regional ITV company or the BBC regional television station but unless you are promoting some community or group enterprise, coverage is unlikely. The Community Programme Unit of the BBC is responsible for *Open Space* which enables groups or individuals to make their own television programme with technical help and advice but in general, television selects its own material and is not open to individual approach.

It is therefore best to concentrate on local radio stations as they can include many more items and a brief, lively broadcast about an exhibition or event can dramatically increase the number of interested visitors. You can get lists of the 27 BBC local radio stations from the BBC and the 43 independent local radio stations from the IBA and then send material (that is, a press release) to those that cover your area. If the material sounds as though it would make a good broadcast, you may well be offered a slot in a news or arts programme. The key to making a success of this is the way you speak. What is required is an enthusiastic, informative and amusing spiel rattling along for the allocated number of minutes. If you do not enjoy talking or do not speak fluently, do not bother to make a broadcast but a natural chatterbox who is not embarrassed can use local radio to increase public interest with one brief broadcast.

The national press

This category consists of the major newspapers, the 'Sundays', the dailies both national and London, and anyone can make a list of the art critics for each of these and compile a mailing list. But is it worth it? You almost might as well post a press release to the moon, almost but not quite, and this is not to accuse the national critics of negligence at all but simply to acknowledge that they are inundated with bids for their attention. Even if you send them a railway ticket, they will still probably not come to your show in outer Lincolnshire and they are well aware of the limitations on their time. So unless you are doing something quite extraordinary, leave the national critics until you have a gallery which is able to attract them.

But there is another way into the national press if you are prepared to use it. Write to another section of the paper; the Sunday and weekend colour supplements publish all sorts of small pieces on miscellaneous matters and you could be one of them, but they go to press six weeks ahead of publication and editorial decisions are taken from three months ahead so you have to get material to them in good time. The other newspaper sections you could approach are: the education correspondent if you are doing a school mural or residency; the technical correspondent if you are using a material in a new or different way, or the women's page editor if you are a woman and doing anything at all of interest. Often the women's page editors are very bright women who are bored silly with traditional women's matters and would love some variation to present itself.

While the art critic may be fending off material, the other correspondents may be very receptive and it doesn't really matter which page of a paper mentions your work.

Local press

Local newspapers are a category on their own; there are hundreds of them and many, but not all, trivialise and sensationalise what news there is. But some of the Fleet Street stars started in the provinces and it would be worth your while finding out if there are any local correspondents of the calibre and sympathy you need. To an even greater extent on local papers, women's page editors can be intelligent and receptive so use them if at all possible.

Specialist press

This consists of the art and craft periodicals and they are listed in Appendix 2; these are the publications most likely to give you coverage. But if you do achieve a review of your work, you take your chance because it may not be complimentary and this can be upsetting. Strong work tends to divide people, for or against, and critics do not agree. Look at theatre reviews as an example of this so don't be dispirited if reviewers don't like your work; they get very tired and jaded.

There are two monthly publications that carry exhaustive information about all manner of opportunities and articles; one is *Artists Newsletter*, edited by Susan Jones, David Butler and Richard Padwick and costing 75p per issue or £8.50 for an annual subscription. No one wanting to know what is going on in the art world can afford to be without it, and it is complemented by *artyfacts* which is a careers newsheet issued monthly for the Faculty of Art and Design at Brighton Polytechnic. The cost to an individual for ten issues is £6, and it also contains articles for art graduates of all disciplines who are in professional practice. It is edited by Linda Ball who wrote *Careers in Art and Design* for Kogan Page.

As an antidote to the comprehensive listing and airing of current opportunity, advance, retreat and peril in these and other art magazines (listed on page 145), an enterprising new publishing company has emerged called Combined Arts. It produces two publications, and both have four editions each year, edited by Justin Howes. The *Combined Arts Bulletin* gives news of exhibitions and publications concerned with (as it says) the combined arts of our time; *Craft History* is a vehicle for serious writing about the crafts. It is publications such as these that take the decorative arts out of the merchandising remit of the large sales stores and crafts out of the village fête tea tent and accord them the status and study that they merit.

The regional arts associations all produce, albeit intermittently, magazines or newsheets. A problem in considering the RAAs is that they differ greatly. They are all completely independent of one another and everybody else and so you have 13 editorial policies, not one. Find out

what your RAA does and use it. There are instances where the editors
are not as spry as one would wish but since their papers are usually free
hand-outs, they are not prompted by commercial considerations which
can be degrading or enhancing, whichever way you look at it.

Periodicals
There are a great many periodicals produced usually every month,
every two months, or twice a month. A good although incomplete list is
published in the *Writer's and Artist's Year Book* and art periodicals are
listed in *The Artist's Directory*. If you can get a colour spread about your
work in one of the glossy magazines such as *The World of Interiors*, the
Sunday colour supplements or *Crafts*, it can do your career a lot of good.
The monthly non-glossy magazines such as *Art Monthly* or the *Arts Review*
have a specialist readership although not a circulation to compare with
the *Sunday Telegraph*.

Press releases
The first rule with the press is to get your material in on time. Hot news
can be printed as it happens but no one will hold the front page for a
review of your work. For monthly glossy magazines, you should
approach them four months ahead of the event; most RAA papers have
a previous month's copy date (the copy date is the date after which
nothing is accepted or altered) and most newspapers like a few weeks'
warning even though they have a copy date of a few days.

It should go without saying that you send a typed letter briefly stating
the nature of your business, with any enclosures such as an artist's
statement also typed in double spacing; (one word on the artist's
statement: remember you are talking to philistine outsiders, not to
Einstein). Photographs and slides should be labelled as never before or
you will not see them again, and certainly if you don't send return
postage. It is best to send them in transparent wrappers so they can be
seen quickly, or else taped to white card.

Editorial and purchased space
These approaches are designed to attract editorial staff to write
something about you. Alternatively, you can write your own article
about your work, your life style, something that interests you and send
it in, but it should appeal to the magazine or paper in question; tending
to the left or the right, a funny, technical or feminist article will be
rejected by one paper but appeal to another. But all this is editorial
material for which you do not pay.

Alternatively you can purchase space for an advertisement or to
publish a picture and while it is an expensive outlay, it can have good

results. *Arts Review* allows you to buy space for advertising with or without colour (subject to editorial control) as do the other art magazines, so proceed according to your need, your budget and where you are in the country. Once you start preparing publicity material, either for use as a display advertisement or in a publicity hand-out, you need the services of a printer.

Printers

Printers are like computers, put rubbish in and rubbish comes out. The worst printer in the world had to acknowledge that the only thing in his favour was that the print didn't actually fall of the paper; the best printer in the world hasn't been discovered yet, like the meaning of life, but many people search and there are near candidates.

Printers require exact instructions and if they don't get them, they may do the opposite of what you want. Whatever you are having printed, the procedure will be as follows:

1. *Find your printer.* As with everything else, you get what you pay for but printers do specialise, in fine work or colour, quantity or speed, so select the one suitable. If you plan to use a printer more than once, find someone and stay with him so he comes to understand your needs.

2. *Get an estimate or a quotation.* These are not the same, an estimate is what they think it will cost, a quotation is what they will charge you. You can tell a lot about a printer from this so never accept it over the phone but ask for it in writing. Look at the quality of the letterhead; if it is badly drawn and printed, they will not understand your values; also look at the clarity and efficiency of the quotation (or estimate). VAT is chargeable on all publicity material like posters and cards but not on books and catalogues. Make sure this is clear; as well as typesetting and proofing costs and arrangements.

3. When you have selected your printer, *accept the estimate (or quotation) by letter*, as this is a contract (offer and acceptance), and make any necessary proviso such as seeing a proof before the final printing is done.

4. *Schedule.* Ask your printer how long the job will take and then quote it back in your confirming letter. Then you must keep to your copy date but tell your printer that your deadline for delivery is three days ahead of actuality to allow for Murphy's Law.

5. *Presentation of written copy.* Handwritten copy deserves the worst fate possible and the better typed your copy is the better it will be printed. It should be double spaced with a margin each side for

printing instructions and it should preferably be typed by one person, especially if it is a long piece because there are subtle differences in everybody's typing. The typescript should be consistent in its use of capital letters, spelling and punctuation; and even the typing of a list can be done in several ways. Your printer can probably lend you a useful book or leaflet giving the standard forms of instruction (such as the underlining of words which implies italics).

You must specify your typeface from those held by the printer, the sizes of type, any changes for headings, indentings, italics etc, and when your printer has received your typed manuscript with instructions for printing, he will produce long galley proofs. You correct these against your copy of the manuscript and you pay for your mistakes and for any alterations and the printer pays for his. Write your instructions in the margins of the galley proof; at this stage the proof is chopped up and arranged on the page with the pictures (the layout). You can ask to see a proof again just before printing in quantity starts but you have to be prepared to visit the printer at a strange hour like dawn and stand by the press as it whirls ink on to paper. It is very expensive indeed to change anything at this stage.

Design copy and layout

If you are preparing your own design and layout it would be as well to ask a graphic designer who is used to preparing material for printing how to present copy because there are some conventions of presentation that, once understood, make life easier. Your printer will, or should, print according to instructions, but it is not his job to improve things. For example, there was a 35mm slide of a painting that was to be printed on a large poster; the painting was by a very elderly artist and the slide had been taken by a non-professional photographer and, unnoticed by everyone, there was a strip of white masking tape along the bottom of the picture. Printed A1 size, it ruined the whole poster and one entire plate had to be remade. It was the designer's fault, not the printer's, and so the cost of remake was at the designer's expense.

Again, you can and should insist on seeing a proof as a condition of contract and if under these circumstances a printer proceeds and prints and it is not as you wish, he will have to reprint at his expense.

Artists' cards

There are various firms that produce postcards of artists' work but one that is run from a good printing studio and which has stood the test of time is Abacus (Colour Printers) at Lowick in Cumbria. They will produce a minimum of 1000 postcards from a 35mm colour slide of your work for less than £90 provided you give them six weeks' notice. They can work more speedily than this but they charge more accordingly.

Chapter 8

The Market Place

There are basically two market-places where you can sell your work: the specialist network of galleries, fairs, shops and spaces that are professionally well run or otherwise for the showing and sale of art, and then the 'underground' of unusual spaces, offered by fate and grasped by opportunity which artists organise for themselves. We shall deal with the 'establishment' network first.

Professional galleries

The conventional art gallery (conventional in the sense of having walls and a roof and not what they do under it) is likely to be one of three types: municipal, private or commercial, or subsidised. Sometimes subsidy is given to the municipal and commercial galleries and the subsidised ones also undertake some commerce, but these are the basic divisions and the categories reflect their intention and origin.

Municipal galleries
When local authorities were reorganised in 1974, the dozens of Victorian and Edwardian built and endowed museums and art galleries were variously siphoned off by their local authorities into departments such as recreation, leisure, amenities, libraries or education, or left to fend for themselves. This shake-up coincided with the availability on the employment market of graduates from the proliferating history of art and design courses at the new polytechnics and universities whose education was often 'topped up' by one of the also proliferating art/museum management courses. Again during the seventies the Arts Council's Housing the Arts Fund was expanding and it helped many municipal galleries to adapt their premises so that they could show touring and temporary exhibitions to advantage.

This injection of finance for premises with an influx of young and well-educated staff enabled several municipal galleries and museums not only to develop as more efficient receptacles for local and national history but also as galleries for historic, modern, thematic and foreign exhibitions of all sorts. Those galleries that by such political good fortune had received some of these benefits were soon distinguished by the vitality of their programmes; they also remained safe depositories for artefacts consigned by 'insubstantial fashion' to temporary oblivion but which all this energy could rescue; forgotten trends and art forms such as utility furniture or marine paintings could be offered for re-evaluation and appreciation as a self-fertilising benefit and the subsequent range of aesthetic tolerance in the art-loving public of the 1980s is perhaps a tribute to this.

All municipal museums and galleries are listed in the *Museums Association Yearbook* which will be in any reference library. However, it will not tell you what each gallery's policy is on modern art and this you can find better indicated in the *Directory of Exhibition Spaces* which is an invaluable publication for far more than its amazingly thorough lists of every sort of exhibition space. Its new, updated edition contains details of about 2500 galleries in the UK, and no self-respecting artist who wants to show and sell work should be without it. It will not say which municipal galleries and museums have only a few Roman coffins and a stuffed penguin with the wire coming out of its feet, but it will say which ones offer rather more. Those are the ones to watch out for.

Their policy on contemporary arts and crafts varies enormously. Some run a register for any professional artist living within 30 miles and show the work of one of them each month; some have no dealings with local artists but base exhibitions and lectures on their often unique collections; the Bradford Print Biennale is run at Cartwright Hall by the City of Bradford Metropolitan Council, and the Whitworth Museum at Manchester specialises in fabrics, ethnic, ancient and modern. So before you approach a municipal gallery asking for an exhibition, find out its policy and try to link your approach to any aspect of it that is suitable.

For example, a young jeweller who used foil and feathers as her main materials approached a museum that had a collection of Chinese feather jewellery; as a result she was given space for a Christmas display of her work which, while not for sale, directed a lot of custom to her workshop.

Private and commercial galleries

If you are not one of those artists who cannot bear to part with their work but want to sell it without the hassle of marketing it yourself, then find a private gallery that will agree to represent you. This might sound like advice in the 'find a crock of gold' category but there are a lot of private galleries and they need you as much as you need them.

A private gallery is as it says, run on private money, and it makes its money from commercial practice, but apart from the Bond/Cork Street coterie, few of them are money spinners and are run from altruism, not greed. They vary from the Marlborough Gallery, which deals on an international level, to a small concern in tourist toy-town dealing with pictures of harrowing horses and sails in the sunset, but basically they are the same in that if they don't earn, they don't exist. Sometimes one of the RAAs or the Arts or Crafts Council may sponsor a particular enterprise or exhibition and sometimes will offer guarantees against loss. Very occasionally public money has been used to stop a private gallery that does good work from becoming bankrupt, but in general they rely on self-survival. Some specialise in a particular art form, such as Anatol Orient who specialises in pots at his gallery in Portobello Road, London, or the Textiles Gallery (that speaks for itself) in Golden Square, London.

So they have an urgent interest to sell and the difference between their staff and those from a gallery without this necessity is apparent to anyone who wants to buy or needs to sell. The best galleries can effect not a hard sell so much as a cunning one, and in the present circumstances of greater economic need the distaste with which many artists and arts administrators have in the past regarded this is fortunately becoming outdated. This necessity dictates that the gallery owners accept what they think will sell and not only what they like, although some carry work they like too and are prepared to promote it without hope of an early return, on the backs of more saleable stock.

Subsidised galleries

Subsidised galleries are supported totally or in part by their local authority, the RAA, or the Arts or Crafts Council and sometimes by all of them. Some enterprises get funds from the district and county councils, the RAA and all the national funding bodies. These galleries are sometimes a part of an arts centre with facilities for film and performance, like the Arnolfini in Bristol.

It is the subsidised and sometimes the municipal galleries that have the staff and the budget to mount the retrospective and foreign exhibitions, the large competitions and the thematic shows that are now a part of our cultural expectation. Although their budgets are not lavish, they are not on the knife edge of solvency like a lot or even most of the private galleries but they do have an obligation to present exhibitions that are both academic and popular to bring in, and please, the public.

The subsidised galleries are on the look-out for new talent because one day it could be to their credit to have shown the 'new David Hockney' first and the private galleries are on the look-out because aesthetic renown can turn into financial success; and the whole gamut of arts administrators are looking for new talent to lend them reflected glory.

How to approach a gallery

Do not bother to approach any gallery in whatever category until you have some reason, however tenuous, for doing so: that you trained or live nearby, that you have enjoyed exhibitions there in the past, or have bought there or, if there is a permanent collection, that your work has some connection with it. For example, if your work is inspired by Indian miniatures, approach a gallery that specialises in them. It may be just enough for the curator or owner to feel that your approach is specific to them and not an indiscriminate appeal sent to every gallery in the land.

Every gallery curator in the country stands by in the summer of each year for the shower of inadequate letters that mark the graduation of that year's thousand or so art graduates. You must not blame them for picking out the ones they can read and the sensible curriculum vitae and looking at the well presented slides. The need for a well written letter applies here as nowhere else. How to do it is described on pages 67–8.

Consigning work to galleries etc

When you leave work for sale with a gallery, shop or agent, there should be some contractual agreement regarding the terms on which it is left. Many artists leave their work on the most informal and flimsy terms and then have little redress when things go wrong.

Work is usually left under one of three agreements: sale or return, outright purchase, or as part of a stipend agreement.

Sale or return

This is the most usual agreement whereby artists and craftspeople leave work on consignment to be returned if unsold. There should be some form of agreement between the two parties, and this can simply be a receipt given on delivery of the goods and a letter which should have covered the following points:

- Sale price including commission and VAT.
- Date of payment to the artist.
- Return of goods: who collects or pays cost.
- Damage: the condition of the goods should always be checked on delivery and receipted. If goods are subsequently lost or damaged, the agent should tell the artist immediately and pay the artist the price he or she would have received had the item been sold. Problems usually arise in the case of unsold work with minor damage but the artist should also receive a proportion of compensation for this.

Outright purchase

From the artist's or craftsperson's point of view this is the ideal arrangement and, depending on the nature of the work, it should carry the contract of sale described in Chapter 7. Fewer galleries and shops are today able to buy work, which makes the economic expectations of most practising artists even more uncertain.

Stipend agreement

Occasionally a gallery will agree to pay an annual stipend to an artist to allow him or her to work without immediate financial worries. Usually the agreement is flexible but if sales of the artist's work do not match the stipend, then work can be taken to the equivalent value of the difference at the end of the period of agreement. Alternatively, if the work sells in excess of the stipend, further payments can be made to the artist.

Contract for an exhibition

Leaving quantities of work on a sale or return basis is one way to start your professional life, but every artist hopes for better exposure. Suppose that a gallery decides to exhibit your work and this offer is made verbally. While you may be overjoyed, during the subsequent week or so one of you should write to the other party formalising the offer. If a gallery is very busy, it may not write at once, in which case you should write and offer your own terms. But one way or another, you must have a contract for the exhibition and this is not a long, formal document but simply a letter stating terms to which you both agree. It should include:

- Name and address of gallery (you could be put in a non-prestigious annexe).
- Date of proposed show.
- Is it a solo or group show?
- What work is to be exhibited and how late will any alteration be accepted?
- If the work isn't done yet, does the gallery have right of veto?
- Prices of work for the artist. Do you charge VAT?
- Commission to be added by the gallery. Does it charge VAT?
- Is the work for sale or return, or is the gallery buying?
- Date of delivery; date of removal.
- Is the work to be framed, mounted, presented in any way?
- Who displays the exhibition and labels it?
- What arrangements are there for press and other publicity and who pays?
- Who pays for and organises the private view?
- Does the gallery tell the artist who buys the work, and if not, what arrangements are made, if any, for work to be borrowed back in the future?

- What are the insurance arrangements for the work?
- When will the gallery pay the artist?
- Is the work to be taken as it is sold and will replacements be required?
- What will be the fee for exhibiting (worth negotiating even if the AC or RAA aided scheme is not usually applicable)?
- What are the opening hours and invigilation arrangements?
- Remember that the artist retains copyright on sales made unless otherwise negotiated. What is the contract of sale?

Even after all this, things can still go wrong and disputes usually arise because one party or the other expects something to happen that does not. If the press don't review the show, whose fault is it? Were you expecting different or better treatment? It is more likely to be a happy and successful show if everything is sorted out first and if the gallery and the public like you, they will invite you back, and in the manner of all consumer loyalty, people who have bought your work once can turn up again years later and buy again. Make fans, not enemies.

Touring exhibitions

Sometimes a tour of an exhibition including your work is proposed and this is usually by the subsidised or municipal galleries as it can be part of their requirement from the funding bodies to do so.

You will – reasonably – be pleased to be included, but approach the offer with caution. Work deteriorates while on tour because it is handled constantly by people who have little concern for its condition. While the reasons for touring art are impeccable – that is, showing art to a new public and winning a new audience – the reality is that a beautifully prepared show comes back after six months looking as if it has been handled by King Kong after eating hamburgers. Also, after a long tour, the work may not only have deteriorated but also look old-fashioned as you may have developed new work since then. While it is a public-spirited thing to participate in, it brings you no money and it can result in damaged or at least 'tired' work.

However, a touring exhibition can offer an artist the opportunity to visit and talk about the work to 'Friends' of the gallery or to local students for an agreed fee and expenses. This not only makes the artist and the work better known but is an opportunity to check on the work's condition at each venue.

Shops

It may by now have become clear that this book aims to direct its readers to help and advice from two sources: specialist and general. The relevant selling outlets will be on the Crafts Council list of selected galleries and shops, and recommendations by the RAAs and publications such as the *Directory of Exhibition Spaces*. The general information sources are available to anyone endeavouring to make a living from their labours and will include schemes run by the county councils, the RDC, the Department of Trade and Industry, the Department of Employment and, in the field of selling, there are the commercial advertisements for shops, mail order firms and other outlets.

Anyone who is manufacturing something intriguing in quantity should look for shops which specialise in that sort of merchandise.

There are well-known firms such as Liberty's One-Off Shop that you could approach but there are many more which tend to advertise in women's magazines, or the girls' and 'girlie' magazines and the weekend colour supplements' advertisement features. They will not bring you kudos but they will bring sales.

Alternative exhibition spaces

For various reasons you may decide to organise a show of your work yourself or with colleagues. The obvious advantage is that you control matters and do not have to pay a commission, and the disadvantage is that the enterprise is time-consuming. There is an excellent book by Debbie Duffin called *Organising Your Own Exhibition* which is practical and thorough besides being cheap (£3).

Open studio

Some artists, and more usually craftspeople, have a display room or area at their home permanently open to the public. This tends to happen in rural areas where property is cheaper. The advantage is that your work can always be seen as you wish and the disadvantage is that, if it is advertised, you will certainly need planning permission.

But a temporary exhibition, say for 10 days at Christmas, can be a good way to sell work, so that people feel they get to know you better; it is an excellent public relations exercise for art in general and you in particular. A lot of contemporary art suffers from being seen as single rather obscure items but when several examples are seen together and especially in an artist's house where furniture and objects and the general environment give obvious validity to the art produced there, it can make the work more understandable. All art professionals are used to seeing

103

each other's houses but to outsiders a visit can have a real excitement and extend understanding of modern work.

In order to sell from your home you must consider planning permission and insurance. It is wise just to ask your planning officer if there is any objection but probably no formal permission will be needed if sales are temporary or infrequent.

Then there is insurance, not only of your work but of your personal possessions. You may intend only to invite people known to you or impeccable members of the art profession but as soon as the numbers of people in your home increase, inexplicable and unfortunate things happen. Put away your handbag-sized valuables and tell your insurance company. A well-known artist lost a Wedgwood bust and a dozen eggs when he thought he had only invited members of the area art society. So, without losing your faith in human nature, be warned.

One final warning in an attempt to stop history repeating itself: if you are tempted to sell from your home permanently, you will find that selling is a time-consuming and specialist business. It is not easy to tolerate members of the leisured public fiddling around all afternoon and finally not buying your best work. Some sort of agent is a good buffer against such trivialisation.

Public venues

There are spaces and places where your work can be shown to advantage and perhaps for gain and where the public already go, for example, pubs, hotels, restaurants, offices and businesses such as banks, building societies, factories, hairdressers, shops, and every other sort of enterprise that constitutes any town high street. All these are possible display areas where your work could be shown to the advantage also of the host organisation, that is, they all want to attract and please the public. There are also the public institutions such as hospitals, local authority offices, colleges and schools, leisure and sports centres, libraries etc, all of which together may offer a lot of wall space and marbled foyer.

The keynote in getting your work shown in such places is 'mutual benefit'. No matter who eventually decides in each organisation that your work would be a benefit and not a liability, a problem-free arrangement will be the aim. Obviously attractive and easily appreciable work will win here; if your work implies smashing capitalism, don't approach a bank; if you are attacking bourgeois values, avoid a building society; violent art is not wanted in hospitals. Art has a bad image in the popular press and the business people whom you approach in this context may vaguely remember incidents involving piles of bricks, soiled underwear and burning rubber tyres and reasonably want none of it. So ask yourself objectively if your work is suitable for this or that venue and, if it is, aim to please.

Find the right person to deal with and send your impeccable letter with evidence of your work. Say at once what you offer and what you want and make a business proposal: for example, free space for free work, delivery, maintenance, commission to the host on sales etc. This could stand as the basis for a contract later on.

A number of agencies exist to place art in unused spaces in just that way. City Gallery in Milton Keynes was started in 1973 simply to put art into all those miles of new offices and factories being built there and is still going strong. Look to see if any work is displayed in buildings around where you live and there should be a label somewhere saying who the agents were for its placing; then you could contact them, but it does take you back to square one in that you would then share the commission on sale with the agent.

Libraries
Libraries deserve a paragraph to themselves. During the local authority boom of the 1960s and early 70s many authorities rebuilt or refurbished their libraries, often including well-appointed exhibition areas or even galleries. But the recession meant that the programme to make use of them and the versatile staff did not always materialise. This has left many good exhibition areas under-used and any county chief librarian could tell you whether or not these are available.

Hospitals
Similarly some hospitals have a new attitude to decor and rather more than decor; several artist in residence placements have been arranged, often under the auspices of the RAA, and murals, pictures, prints and sculptures have been bought in spite of financial restraints. These arrangements are never simple to effect and can take ages to materialise but the general administrator in each case is the key person.

Independent group shows
People are more likely to see your work if it happens to be displayed at a place they visit for other purposes. The public tread an unvarying path and when Richard Buckle put on a major show of Epstein's work in a greyhound racing stadium in Edinburgh in the 1950s, public attendance outstripped all expectation because everyone was used to going there and didn't mind so much what for.

If you hang your work in the library, lots of people will see it; with what attention is another matter. But if you hold an exhibition somewhere that only the dedicated will find, they will give it their full attention once they arrive. An existing audience may give cursory attention but a 'purpose formed' audience will try harder.

Suppose a group of like-minded artists decide to run an exhibition of work that will also be for sale and set about finding premises. The advertisement columns of the local paper are a good start, asking the property department of the local authority, notes in newsagents' windows, word of mouth or, as is suggested in Chapter 5, cycling along looking for abandoned premises. The use of local information sources combined with perseverance and guile will probably win in the end. An exhibition can be organised anywhere but for people to come it must be reasonably accessible and if it is upstairs, the audience will drop at once.

So, once you have found your suitable warehouse/barn/village or school hall/empty church/shop/factory/garage, you assess what needs to be done to it. Depending how many of you there are, allocate the tasks.

- Who is in charge, a committee or one person?
- Where does the money to run this come from (you may get paid back)?
- Do you need to clean/paint/prepare the premises?
- Equipment: what about lighting, tables, plinths etc?
- Who selects exhibits and allocates space?
- Who deals with advertising, talks to local radio (see Chapter 7)?
- Who acts as treasurer, handles money 'in' and money 'out'?
- Will you open a special bank account?
- Will you set up a rota of supervisors once the show is on?
- Who is in charge of exhibits, lists, insurance and stock control?

One unavoidable characteristic of a show like this is that it will take a great deal of everybody's time; an avoidable characteristic is that everybody falls out because responsibilities are not clearly divided and everyone feels that he or she alone carried the whole burden. But if it is well done, the participants *can* make some money and make the community aware of their presence.

Festivals, fairs and markets

Nothing shows up more clearly the different attitudes of the various service organisations than how they advertise events such as these. The specialist and up-market craft fairs will be advertised by the Crafts Council whose aim is to promote nationally the best creative crafts. A great number of crafts fairs are listed in the *Craftsman's Directory* which comes out once a year when, by the nature of things, many dates and details are not available and it gives no grade of quality. The local authorities will know what is going on in their areas but they are not given to making quality assessments, but the regional arts associations by contrast have a requirement of quality for the rather more esoteric events, and only an RAA could promote 'fringe puppetry' but their advertisement of events varies among the 13 associations. The Scottish Development Agency promotes the development of crafts in Scotland and basically operates in the same manner as the Crafts Council. The RDC which also covers counties will have politely little time for non-commercial, experimental work that is the *raison d'être* of the RAAs and this is not to ignore the local arts councils and associations who run their own festivals and fairs. There are also the specialist groups such as potters' groups and the Embroiderers' Guild and Fibre Art who can give excellent support to their members and run splendid fairs. The Rural Crafts Association is helpful also on fairs for mainly rural crafts and in Wales there is the Welsh Crafts Council which is a membership organisation for running fairs and giving services and advice. One of the most lively arts festivals is the Oxfordshire Visual Arts Festival which now runs its own news sheet to advertise the open studios, exhibitions and many other activities that now merit national advertising.

The biggest open annual painting fair is the Royal Academy summer exhibition and the Royal Over-Seas League also runs an annual exhibition, but artists are limited by age as they must be under 35. For five years the Contemporary Art Society has held an invited art market at Smith Gallery in Covent Garden and the Athena Art Awards are also by invitation. The International Contemporary Art Fair is held most years at London Olympia and consists mainly of stalls taken by galleries or organisations to show the work of the artists in their 'stable'. Another Contemporary Art Fair is held at Bath. To really know what is going on in time to participate you will need an eye in every direction.

Outdoor sites

Exhibition or selling outlets such as Camden Lock Market and the railings of Hyde Park in London are usually strictly controlled and you cannot go along and set out your wares on impulse. If you want to take part, you can find who is responsible either by asking other stall holders or, if they will not tell you (and you will immediately represent competition) you can ask the local authority of the area. Sometimes these venues are run by private individuals or by some form of business or by the local authority itself, but the local authority will know because it will have granted planning permission, even if only to itself. If the authority will not divulge the relevant name and address, it will forward a letter;

107

you can find out which local authority is responsible from the nearest post office.

One of the most interesting agencies for outdoor site commissioning is Common Ground which is run from the London Ecology Centre. Their *New Milestones Project* aims to commission small-scale sculptures which reflect the character of the place in which they are sited, in the tradition of the old milestones, and to involve the local community in selecting the artist and enabling the sculpture to evolve. Environmental concerns in the materials used, the forms portrayed and the sites selected are a feature of several modern commissioning agents which seek to unite artistic and environmental concerns.

Competitions

Most fairs and markets are for crafts of one sort or another but most competitions are for traditional fine arts. They are expensive and time-consuming to run so they are usually promoted by one of the subsidised or municipal bodies; the Tolly Cobbald Eastern Arts Show has been run for several years by Eastern Arts with sponsorship by the Tolly Cobbald Brewery but its future at present seems to be uncertain. The Turner Prize is run by the Tate and the John Moores Liverpool Exhibition was run from 1957-1987 by the Walker Art Gallery, while the John Player Portrait Award is run each year by the National Portrait Gallery. All these will be advertised in the relevant press, that is relevant in type and level (horses for courses).

Once you send for and receive the details, two things may strike you. One is the list of rules and regulations that may seem petty and endless and the other is the hanging fee. The fee is simply prompted by the expense of the whole operation that is not designed to make money, and the rules will have been written by someone who has in the past suffered everything going wrong that can do so. So if the rules specify a maximum size for work, it is because there is a door somewhere of that size; if there is a maximum weight, it is because that is what the staff can carry. Do try and co-operate with the organiser because even the most dedicated can become exasperated and you don't want it to be your work that is left until the judges are tired, or displayed on the stairs in a bad light.

When it comes to judging the winners, the same impossible criteria apply as in awarding grants etc. It is partly luck, of a sort, because the decisions are subjective, so if you don't like or trust the judges, don't enter.

Chapter 9

The Financial Gap

This chapter refers to the gap between what you earn and what you need. Howard Hughes is reputed to have said that 'Your net income should meet your gross habits' and, while you will probably not have time or energy for many really gross habits, the principle is sound.

Most professional people accept that some financial hardship is likely in the early stages of their careers but some careers or 'callings' carry this likelihood throughout a lifetime. Most of the arts come into this category and this book aims to help artists make the best of the situation. This can be done partly by careful handling of business matters and partly by taking up the specialist and general opportunities that exist. The already difficult situation has been exacerbated by the current economic trend whereby the poor have tended to get poorer and the financial gap for many is widening.

If your financial gap widens too far, life will not cease but it can become very uncomfortable. But there are ways of earning extra income which can improve your circumstances when times are bad and, while some have been touched on elsewhere, you may find it useful to have them summarised and to be introduced to a few new ones as well.

Social security

When you are self-employed you will not be eligible for unemployment benefit but you may be able to claim income support. This is dealt with in detail in Chapter 2, but you are reminded of it here as it can act as a financial safety net when all else fails.

Collect money owing to you

Those who owe you money are your debtors; those to whom you owe money are your creditors. It is in your financial interest to fend off your creditors as long as possible and equally in your interest to receive money owing promptly. Money that remains with your debtors is probably earning them interest and at your expense if you are paying interest on an overdraft. Ways to chase debtors are dealt with in Chapter 4, but the point needs to be made that to chase and receive money owing to you could help to fill your yawning gap.

Use a professional skill

If you are trained, professional artist you will have a number of skills that could be turned to financial account. You may feel reluctant to do this because it will deplete your time and energy available for other matters but it can be done in a financial emergency. The sort of money earning activities for which you may be well suited might include:

- The professional use of equipment (such as cameras or videos).
- The offering of a professional service and advice such as decor, decoration or exhibition work, or general services such a cooking, typing, sewing or removal work.
- The extension of your professionalism into other areas such as modelling or writing.

An example of this concerns a fine art student who graduated from one of the Midland art colleges and, as part of his course, had been taught to use cameras and video equipment. On leaving college he found himself as ill-equipped as his contemporaries to earn a living. Trying to survive as a freelance artist but needing to earn money, he wrote to the 15 newspapers and magazines which had offices within 20 miles of his home offering his services as a photographer. As a result, two papers commissioned him to send them each week contact sheets of his general photographs, taken during his daily life, and they bought, on average, two per fortnight. Since it was horse-riding and hunting country and he was particularly interested in speed and the vision of speed, he came to specialise in horse photography for which the county magazines paid well.

There are many such examples but it has tended to be unfashionable to admit to these fringe activities. A graphics graduate who set up as a freelance designer straight from college decided to keep a watchful eye on all the shop fronts and windows in the town area where she lived in case any design opportunities presented themselves. She approached a local garage when it changed hands to ask for a commission for a special window display both for Christmas and to advertise their new range of services. A fee of £500 plus £500 for materials was agreed; the work took about a month and involved dealing with the local planning department over setting up a Christmas tree outside the garage, and also the fire risk of having decorations inside the garage, and it was deemed to be a success. Her name was advertised as a part of the commission and she was retained on an annual basis for the Christmas display.

These money-making forays into new areas of activity need not be confined to your specialism and after four years of higher education, you might reasonably regard yourself as a versatile creature who is ready for anything. A fine art graduate who had always enjoyed writing approached several specialist art magazines as well as local papers with examples of her exhibition and book reviews. These were each attuned to the paper concerned, ie a short and slightly jokey review for the local paper, and a serious review of the right average length for the specialist magazines, but all were well typed on plain paper in double spacing with a stamped, addressed envelope for their return and a brief, courteous letter introducing herself. As a result, the local paper commissioned her to write a review of an exhibition about three times a year and one of the major papers commissioned her the following summer to review the major art colleges final degree shows, paying her expenses and offering a fee.

The principle of these three examples (and there are many more) is that somewhere there is a demand for the professional skills an artist has to offer. When offering any service, bear in mind the circumstances of the people whom you contact; do not approach a busy trading firm on Saturday or an office on Friday afternoon; present what you have to offer clearly with well developed and printed photographs labelled on the back or a correctly typed script with perfect grammar, double spacing and a word count at the end. A courteous letter can help to indicate whether you are pleasant to have around and it is important to suggest subtly that you will also be useful, that is, can you drive, type, use a camera?

These three artists made the first move by letter or in person. No one is bound to receive an unsolicited approach, so while gallery owners or business people may seem arrogant in their refusal to see you, it is their prerogative. Unsolicited material sent through the post does not have to be returned or even opened, but since everyone is always on the look-out for talent, it probably will be considered. However, if it was not invited, its return is courtesy only and the enclosure of an SAE encourages this. If and when you are rejected, do not be aggrieved, or if you are, do not show it.

If you do enter the periphery of an alternative career, two things will save you a lot of time: one is to talk to someone already in practice as a writer or photographer or whatever and ask them some very basic questions, and the other is to find the relevant journals or publications pertaining to it. For example, if you are considering writing reviews or fiction, the national publications are listed in the *Writers' and Artists' Year Book* and it is advisable to select all the relevant ones and send them each a photocopy of your work with, of course, a personal letter. The reason for this is that you can wait three months for a journal to tell you they don't take that sort of work whereas if you send it to four in the first place, you are not so likely to waste time and you enhance your chances of success.

Part-time and temporary work

Teaching has been the most usual part-time work for artists but the recent education cuts have made it more difficult to find – difficult but not impossible – so if you intend to teach, it would be as well to obtain teaching qualfications because you need them to teach in primary or secondary schools. You do not need qualifications to teach in higher or futher education, strange as this may seem, but you will be more likely to get teaching work if you are qualified. Teaching posts are advertised in *The Times Educational Supplement*.

Primary and secondary school supply teaching is always available, even today, and any part-time or temporary work can produce income: the problem then is the way in which you are paid as a self-employed person. If you are paid gross, then provided you declare it for income support (if you are drawing it) and also when you come to do your income tax returns, there is no problem. Any expenses associated with the job such as overalls and travel can, of course, be set against the eventual tax.

However, if you are taken on to the payroll as an employee on PAYE, whether part-time or temporary your National Insurance contribution and income tax will be deducted from your pay. If you are already paying your own National Insurance contribution you will find that you are doing so twice, and at different grades. You will not be entitled to have the second payment refunded and the period of work may be too short for it really to be worth your while to adjust your own payments. This period of employment will interrupt your self-employment record and you may find the net payments very low over a short period; they are a better option over a longer time span. If you apply for income support when you leave, you will not be eligible for six weeks because you have been employed and not self-employed.

Work out carefully if short-term employment is financially worth it. Often it is not, which is the reason why supply teachers are hard to find.

There are other sorts of temporary work, sometimes because economic cuts have reduced the permanent staff of many organisations so that when a special project is planned, such as an exhibition or a festival, it is advantageous to employ a temporary consultant. Another reason is that statutory maternity leave means that eligible career women are entitled to leave their jobs when pregnant for six months and then return afterwards. If and when this is extended to paternity leave this opportunity for interesting temporary work will expand.

When you apply for such jobs, the key is to convince the potential employer that you will fit in with the existing team and that you will be useful. This unavoidable dictate applies also to permanent jobs, as it is often not the best and most brilliant candidate who is appointed but the one who will fit in best with the existing team. With a temporary job especially the employers are not looking for uncomfortable brilliance but professional trustworthiness.

Subsidy and sponsorship

The network of national, regional and local subsidising bodies can seem complex but it has a logic of a sort which, once understood, could benefit your career. The system is described fully in Chapter 10 but the general advice is not to see it as a means of solving long-term financial problems but rather as a system that could include you in a professional network of like-minded people.

Loans

If any of the subsidising bodies do give money, while it may be in return for work or services, it will almost certainly not be repayable; it is in the manner of a gift (even with strings attached) and not a loan except for a system run by the Welsh Arts Council. Few of the other subsidising bodies give loans because the administrative procedures necessary to claim them back are prohibitive in their usually rather small organisations, but there are exceptions to this. Grants are financially better than loans because loans cost money in interest since you are buying the convenience of the money you borrow. The advertisements on television which ask 'Could you use £5000 right now?' do not so clearly tell you details of what it will cost you and such advertisements, however persuasive, are prompted by profit and not altruism. See Chapter 4 for further information.

Summary

A summary of ways to supplement your income while pursuing your creative work might include:

- Claim social security.
- Collect any money owing to you.
- Use a professional skill.

- Part-time and temporary work.
- Seek subsidy and/or sponsorship.
- Apply for loans.

None of these need distract you from your main purpose but they could fend off an uncomfortable degree of financial need and could lead to new and useful contacts and opportunities.

Chapter 10

The Art Subsidy Network

The art subsidy bodies are organised in three tiers, national, regional and local, a similar pattern to government which is organised on national, county and district levels. The national bodies are the Arts Council of Great Britain, the Welsh Arts Council, the Scottish Arts Council, the Arts Council of Northern Ireland, the Crafts Council, the British Film Institute and the British Council – and it is logical also to include the Design Council although it is not strictly a subsidising body. The regional bodies are the 13 English and three Welsh regional arts associations. Scotland does not have these regional bodies in the same way but the equivalent amount of money per capita is distributed by the local authorities and the Scottish Arts Council. On a local level, there are the local arts councils and associations whose coverage of the country is uneven and which deal mainly with the amateur arts.

Services offered

One warning note should be sounded concerning applications by individuals for grants etc, which is that out of the many thousands of full-time, professional, self-employed and creditable artists and craftspeople between the ages of 20 and 80, only a small proportion of them will receive grants at any time in their careers; this is mainly because there isn't unlimited money to go round and grant-aided individuals is not a current priority, as it is generally much preferred to help groups. Also some sorts of work and some sorts of applicants remain strangely unlucky and to an extent, getting a grant is sheer luck. Do not rely on it and, even if you do, unless it is a residency of some sort, it will probably only solve a short-term problem, not a long-term difficulty.

A great deal of time can be saved and disappointment avoided if you find out first to whom you should apply for what and not send pointless applications to the wrong people. A lot of bureaucrats in general and art bureaucrats in particular spend time forwarding applications to each other because the client has not understood the system first. It is not endlessly complicated and for individual artists and craftspeople trying to get some help, the procedure is explained for each body mentioned in this chapter.

There should at some point be a word generally about bureaucrats and officials, who are the appointed staff not the elected members of an official body, whether you are dealing with the Arts Council or a district planning department. There is no universal description to be given of them and no one official can represent a whole organisation, so while the RAA officer may be very helpful in one town, his or her counterpart may be quite different in another, and while there may be a patient planning officer in one part of the country, there may be a mean man elsewhere. Most officials are anxious for reasonable clients and a quiet life, according to their job they will be more or less interested in you but there is very little redress against them if you feel they are negligent as their superiors will support them, at least in public. If you really have a genuine grievance against an official of a public body, you can write to a senior officer or to an elected representative of that body who may be more responsive as he or she relies for power on your vote, but any complaint has to be very well substantiated.

National bodies

Arts Council of Great Britain
The Arts Council is the longest established of the national organisations and was founded as a permanent body in 1946 with a Royal Charter which was finalised in its present state in 1967. It developed from the wartime CEMA (Council for the Encouragement of Music and the Arts) which had endeavoured to maintain and develop some vestige of national cultural life during the war.

The Council has long outgrown its humble beginnings and its income for 1986/87 was in excess of £128 million. This is allocated by the government of the day through Parliament but the significance of the Royal Charter is that the legal authority and existence of the Council is dependent on the Crown and not on Parliament. The independent status of the Arts Council as a non-political organisation depends on this separate authority and while Parliament can exert financial pressure on the Council, it cannot legally assert political interference.

The objects of the Arts Council are:

● To develop and improve the knowledge, understanding and practice of the arts;
● To increase the accessibility of the arts to the public throughout Great Britain;
● To advise and co-operate with government departments, local authorities and other bodies to achieve these objects.

How well or otherwise it fulfils these objects and how much money

Parliament votes it for the work are the issues so often discussed in the press.

Its status is that of an independent charity with public accountability for its expenditure. Its annual reports and its accounts in a separate booklet are widely distributed to all the local authorities and every county library.

The Arts Council no longer makes grants to individual artists because responsibility for these has been handed over to the RAAs under a national agreement of devolution. It is understandable that more kudos is felt to be attached to a grant from a national rather than a regional body where you may feel in too great proximity to the people making the decisions. But devolution to the RAAs has been achieved in every area of arts subsidy because it was believed the RAAs were in a better position to know and understand the needs of their immediate clients.

The Arts Council nowadays has little direct dealing with artists and indeed states in its 1986-87 Annual Report, 'The Arts Council, of course is not in business to run a lifeboat service for artists in distress'. Subsidy for the individual has been handed over to the now complete network of regional arts associations, but one of the very few remaining schemes whereby the Arts Council directly assists the artist is in purchasing work.

The Arts Council's own promotions have also been either discontinued, like its shop and its poetry library, or else a new authority has been created, as in the case of the South Bank Board that now runs the Hayward Gallery and all touring exhibitions, formerly the responsibility of the art department. The Serpentine Gallery is also now a separate entity and both it and the South Bank Board are clients of the Arts Council.

The Hayward Gallery and the Serpentine were both initiated by the Arts Council, but have been reformed as independent clients because it has been decided that it is inappropriate for any of the subsidy bodies to undertake their own promotions.

Basically the argument has been that while any of the subsidy bodies fund their own promotions, whether galleries, theatres or art centres, they will be their own largest client. In a time of economic growth, this is acceptable to everyone but in a time of financial restriction, other clients who are denied the funds they ask for can (and do) accuse the subsidy bodies of favouring themselves. This concern has gathered such momentum that all the subsidy bodies are preparing to discontinue their own schemes and channel the diminishing funds towards their most deserving clients.

The Arts Council's visual arts expenditure is now devoted to a number of independent galleries (such as the Oxford Museum of Modern Art), some of the municipal galleries (such as the Castle at

Nottingham) and two magazines: *Exhibition Bulletin* and *Performance*. Assistance is also on offer for exhibitions, providing they have a national relevance or are to tour nationally for the production of artists' book-works and for surveys, research or conferences that contribute to areas of current debate in the arts. Major fellowships and residencies such as that run annually at the National Gallery are still Arts Council inspired and subsidised, and there is a new scheme aimed to enlarge the provision of exhibitions of work by black artists under the 'Black Visual Arts Exhibition Franchises'.

Purchasing is perhaps the most direct way the Arts Council aids artists at present but its future is currently under discussion. The Collection was started in 1942 and now comprises over 7000 items; it is impeccably catalogued in a publication appropriately called *Arts Council Collection* with an updating *Acquisitions 1979-83*. It has no permanent display space in London so one might well wonder what is done with it. It is sent out in four to eight touring exhibitions a year and various items are lent to over 80 towns each year. Occasionally at least a sample of the complete collection is shown, but in general it is widely scattered.

A number of schemes that were carefully devised during the late 1970s by the Arts Council with the regional arts associations have now been fully devolved to the RAAs and, in the nature of things, have developed discrepancies across the 13 bodies that implement them. These schemes are all the grant-aid schemes and the Exhibition Payment Right, Works of Art for Public Spaces and studio grants. Purchasing, assisted purchase and residencies are all described in the annual reports of the 13 RAAs. It all may seem very complicated and a long way from an artist who simply needs some money. Part of the answer is that the RAAs have taken over the grass-roots level of subsidy from the Arts Council, leaving the Arts Council with the more esoteric schemes; also, many of these schemes are devised to attract matching money from some other sources. Finally, it is in the nature of bureaucracies to become more complicated rather than less, and this is partly explained by the larger sums of money involved as time goes on and partly to combat genuine complexities that develop.

One of these joint national and regional schemes, *Payment for Exhibiting*, should be emphasised as being of particular relevance to the individual artist. All these joint schemes have varied success as they depend on the conviction with which they are applied to different or even incongruous situations, and the flexibility with which they are administered. The Welsh Arts Council has applied this scheme to the benefit of its artists with customary vigour and is aiming to increase the current payment and involve the galleries in a contribution. But the message to the individual is that if you hold a solo or two-person show, ask your RAA about this payment as it is just possible that it may not be brought to your attention.

A detailed account of the comparative funding between the national and regional bodies is made in the Gulbenkian Foundation survey *The Economic Situation of the Visual Artist* and readers who wish to know more should consult it. It is appropriate here only to give the basic facts.

Welsh Arts Council and Scottish Arts Council

When the Arts Council's Charter was revised in 1967, the Welsh and Scottish committees were discontinued and instead two national arts councils were set up, one to operate for Wales from Cardiff and one for Scotland from Edinburgh.

Both the Scottish and the Welsh Arts Councils receive their money from the Arts Council and they are each run by an appointed Council with advisory panels for each of the arts, and specialist officers. They both bear a greater similarity to the Arts Council than they do to even the largest RAA, partly in terms of their finance in relation to the population and partly because they each deal with a country defined by geography, history and nationalism. They both know whom they serve and it is a clearly defined population that is small enough for an arts council with an adequate budget to be able to make a cultural impact.

Welsh Arts Council

Wales is strongly affected by the existence of a living, national language other than English. The need to serve these two cultures allows extra finance so that, for example, the Welsh Arts Council's Annual Report is published in Welsh and English, the Literature Department has a Welsh section and Wales is in every sense a bilingual country with the complication and the richness that this brings.

The Welsh Arts Council became particularly well-regarded in the 1960s and 70s for its exhibitions which included the *Art and Society* series. But in common with the Arts Council and some of the RAAs, the Welsh Arts Council has, under increasing budget restrictions, had to make the choice between its own promotions and enabling clients to develop their own programme. Therefore, funding priority has been diverted from its own exhibitions to establish a countrywide Exhibition Service with advice, co-ordination and transport on offer. Oriel gallery and bookshop are still directly funded and Collectorplan has replaced direct purchasing by the Council. This is a scheme whereby interest-free loans are offered to individuals buying works of art so that they can pay gradually over a period of time. It is operated from 30 selected galleries and in the first year of operation, 300 works were bought by loan and the repayments collected so that the scheme is almost self-financing and has clearly boosted sales of art that is mainly destined to hang in private homes.

Schemes to help individuals include interest-free loans, and residencies, and new travel and master class schemes are being initiated. Crafts are administered by the Welsh Arts Council and include special projects grants and awards beside residencies, and the new Showcase Network has been developed to show the work of contemporary craftspeople to a new audience.

Scottish Arts Council
The Scottish Arts Council differs from WAC in that it has no regional arts associations and neither does it subsidise crafts. This is dealt with by the Scottish Development Agency. Otherwise, its pattern of subsidy is not dissimilar from the other national arts councils or the largest of the RAAs, Northern Arts, which it borders. It undertakes no direct promotions but subsidises galleries and exhibitions throughout Scotland. It still compiles touring exhibitions but this policy is under review as is its own art collection for which it has been purchasing since its inception. Commissions, awards, bursaries and residencies are available to individual artists on application and there is a system of purchases and assisted purchases.

Arts Council of Northern Ireland
The Arts Council of Northern Ireland is funded directly by the Department of Education for Northern Ireland. Its visual arts policy includes grants and guarantees to artists and arts activities and it subsidises galleries and exhibitions throughout the province. Subsidy of crafts has not been extensively developed but it is handled by the Local Enterprise Development Unit.

Crafts Council
The provision for the visual arts as it evolved under the Arts Council in general excluded the crafts. This was because in the 1940s there were fewer creative craftspeople and the term 'crafts' implies so many facets that are difficult to evaluate in aesthetic terms, such as rural crafts, traditional crafts, utility crafts and technical crafts. But over the last two decades there has been a great development of the experimental and creative crafts and this is largely due to the expansion and reorganisation of art education with new courses that both employ and produce new craftspeople. It was to offer this expanding profession the services of subsidy that the Crafts Council was formed in 1971. Its original name was the Crafts Advisory Committee and this was changed in 1979 to the Crafts Council when it received its Royal Charter.

In common with the other subsidising bodies, it is a registered charity and its Council is appointed by the Minister for the Arts. It receives its income annually through Parliament with the direction to spend it on support for the crafts in England and Wales, and this includes many schemes to help the individual.

The Crafts Council is sensitive to the needs of individual craftspeople as the nature of craftsmanship demands a high level of personal commitment. It operates the following schemes:

Exhibitions, of which about eight of historic and contemporary work are held each year at the Crafts Council Gallery in Waterloo Place, and a number of small 'sideshows' are held at the ICA in the Mall.

The Craft Shop in the Victoria and Albert Museum is run by the Crafts Council and provides a retail outlet for contemporary crafts.

Information is run from the floor above the Gallery and is an archive of material about the practitioners and circumstances of crafts in the country. Primarily it consists of the Register, which is a record of every craftsperson known to the Council, and the Index which is an illustrated record of selected craftspeople.

A collection has been made since 1973 of contemporary crafts in the same way as other national collections. It was exhibited in its near entirety in 1985 but is normally used for loans or assembled into small, touring exhibitions.

Publications include the bimonthly *Crafts* magazine and substantial surveys, such as *Working in Crafts* and smaller publications.

Education and training schemes are run for specific crafts, for recent graduates or people setting up a workshop.

For the individual, the following grants are on offer:

Setting-up scheme comprises an equipment grant and/or a maintenance grant and is for people who have set up a workshop in the last two years.

Training scheme enables craftspeople to obtain practical workshop experience before setting up their own workshop.

Advanced training to enable craftspeople to extend their training.

Loan scheme, a facility whereby up to £5000 is lent at an interest rate of 10 per cent.

Bursary scheme to enable established craftspeople to take a year's sabbatical leave for study or to develop new work.

121

All these applications carry their own conditions and criteria and all applications are assessed by committee.

The Design Council

The Design Council is not a subsidising body in the same way as the Arts Council or Crafts Council for its purpose is 'to promote' by all practical means the improvement of design in the products of British industry. It receives its income from the Department of Trade and Industry but earns almost as much again from its publications, sponsored projects and promotions. It is useful to the individual practitioner for its bookshop, its design and technical advisory service, its design index of consumer and contract goods selected for their design and its promotion of the work of selected designers. It has a specific Welsh presence, office, showroom etc, and a special Welsh Design Award.

The British Council

To complete the list of national councils relevant to artists, it must be mentioned that the British Council exists to promote British interests and culture abroad just as the Arts Council exists to promote them within this country. The British Council has an active fine arts department which purchases work and promotes exhibitions, usually in response to specific requests from overseas institutions. Sometimes they compile an exhibition in collaboration with one of the other subsidy bodies and the paint and textile exhibition 'Fabric and Form' was a joint exhibition with the Crafts Council. There is also a scheme whereby artists who have been invited to exhibit abroad can apply for help with the associated costs involved, but these grants are competitive because the proposed show has to coincide with current Council policy in that particular country.

Regional and local bodies

Local authorities

Because there is a certain amount of arts expenditure by the local authorities and because the regional arts associations rely for a proportion of their income on them, it is necessary here to give a brief description of their organisation.

The country is divided into geographical counties each of which is administered by an elected county council. There are 47 English and Welsh shire counties. The shire counties are further divided into over 300 districts, all being administered by elected councils. The counties and districts have different levels of responsibility, both having appointed full-time officers to carry out the duties and policies of the elected members; for example, the planning and building regulations officers will be based at the district council but the County Courts, education and library service will be run by the county council. Occasionally districts are called boroughs but this is only tradition.

Apart from a different legal system, Scotland also has its own local authority structure with ten regional and one Highlands and Islands authorities.

All these authorities are intended to be permanent and it takes an Act of Parliament to rearrange them. But there are also the development corporations which are set up for a specific period of time to fulfil a particular purpose such as to build a new town or redevelop an area. They have vested in them many of the powers normally held by the county or district authority, such as compulsory purchase and planning. Once they have completed their task, they hand over these powers and are disbanded. Thus the Milton Keynes Development Corporation was set up to build the new city of Milton Keynes and, when its work is complete, a new local authority will be formed to assume the powers of local government. Merseyside Development Corporation was instigated to redevelop parts of derelict Liverpool and it was responsible for the Liverpool Garden Festival in 1984 which was really a land reclamation exercise rather than just a garden festival. The new Development Areas (eg Docklands) are, to an extent, usurping their role.

The significance of this identification of local government is that many of the counties and development corporations have an arts policy and are appointing specialist art staff. Either they collaborate with the RAAs or they have their own arts and leisure departments which appoint artists in residence in schools and hospitals, buy work such as the Leicestershire Education Authority's art collection, commission and buy public sculpture as does the Milton Keynes Development Corporation or run art and crafts centres such as the Rufford Craft Centre in north Nottinghamshire. Arts expenditure is very varied but you can find out if your county is active in this area by checking in the *Municipal Year Book* which lists all local authorities and their departments and staff.

If you are self-employed it will also be helpful to understand the nature of the parish councils. They are based upon historic land division and are only found in rural areas and, while they are elected, they do not usually have paid full-time staff. They receive modest funds, mainly from the district council, and they fulfil some statutory obligations but they act essentially in a consultative capacity. The town councils are similar in scope and authority and they will both certainly be involved in planning permission for a new 'light industry', so look on the local post office notice board for their details.

Regional arts associations

The 1950s and 60s were a time of considerable local authority expansion and arts funding was one of many new areas of development. As neighbouring county councils across the country collaborated in groups of four or five and offered a financial commitment to arts funding, so the Arts Council, and later the other national bodies, offered money to the regional groupings on the 'pound for pound' principle. To receive and spend this double purse the regional arts associations were founded with the intention that they would fund the arts of their region independently of the political nature of the national government or of the funding counties or local districts which also contributed to them.

There are now 13 regional arts associations and they are commonly called collectively the 'RAAs'. The earliest was founded in 1956 and the most recent in 1984 and they vary enormously in size, population and income and the nature and variety of their activities reflect these differences. Their names and territories are listed in Appendix 1.

Several of the RAAs have now dropped the word 'association' from their title but this is only for brevity of expression. Try to recognise an RAA when you meet one. When you are deciding where to live (see Chapter 5), one factor could be the quality and nature of the relevant RAA, and wherever you live there will be a visual arts officer whose job it is to have some concern for your professional welfare. A long-established officer who has had the trust of successive advisers will wield a lot of influence, but a new officer may have very little; either way their role is to persuade and advise rather than to exercise authority.

The RAAs have basically the same structure and status as the national arts bodies. They are all independent charities with public accountability for their expenditure. During the 1970s there were considerable similarities between their structures and procedures but, as they have become better established organisations (and only one RAA has ever actually been disbanded and then it was reformed rapidly) and so have related more accurately to their region, they have become very different from each other. For example, Northern Arts is the oldest, the largest and the wealthiest and is more like an 'Arts Council' of the north, whereas Buckinghamshire Arts is the newest and smallest, operating only for Buckinghamshire and legally a client of East Midlands Arts. Lincolnshire and North Humberside Arts has a largely rural region while Greater London Arts consists of the 32 London boroughs. It is therefore impossible to give an accurate, generalised account of their policies and procedures; originally they all operated by a system of advisory panels which decided the criteria whereby grant aid should be given and recommended who should receive it. Some of the RAAS still operate this system (presumably because it works well) but some have renamed their panels 'working groups' and some have a series of specialist advisers who are consulted individually for smaller grants and major decisions are made by the governing body, usually called the Executive Committee.

Applying for subsidy
You should apply to the RAA to which your county council contributes and your county is the one to which you pay rates. If you live on a county border, it is not your postal address that determines your placing but where you pay your general rates.

All the RAAs produce pamphlets, newsheets and bulletins that are usually distributed in libraries and information centres and they will carry their address and phone number. If you cannot find this publication, then ask your district or county council who and where your RAA is and go up the scale of seniority until you find someone who knows. The RAAs are also listed in major art directories. There should be a copy of the RAA's annual report in the main reference library and in this you will find as much about the RAA as any publication will tell you. But there will also be the facts that any public body is bound to publish.

- How much total income they received and from where
- What it was spent on
- Who made the decisions
- Who carried them out.

Then there will be a section on Visual Arts either separately or together with Crafts and Photography, and from this you can find out what sort of money they have to spend and what they spend it on. The categories will probably include:

Art galleries and art centres
Exhibitions, static and touring
Organisations, studios, groups
Artists in residence
Special events, festivals, performances, workshops
Payment for exhibitors
Art for public places
Commissions and purchases
Art publications
Artists' index
Grants/loans to individuals

The main trend by the RAAs is to give less money to individual artists simply to produce work. Grants are harnessed far more to commissions (and are often 50 per cent of the total cost, the rest to be made up by the commissioning body) or to studios, equipment and facilities for a group.

Most of the RAAs, and especially those dealing with large, metropolitan areas, are developing into planning and development agencies for the arts, persuading the local authorities and other large bodies to spend money on art works and then facilitating purchase and commission. One successful example of this is the iron horses by Kevin Atherton that are situated along the railway line between Birmingham and Wolverhampton, an instance of imaginative collaboration between West Midlands Arts and British Rail. The RAAs have experience and they know the artists of their region; while they have low budgets in any commerical sense, they are important catalysts which should direct the artist, lost in a maze of bureaucracy and hampered by poverty, to the most relevant studio, grant, loan or agency.

However, most of the RAAs make some grants to individuals so since this book is for the individual struggling to make a living, this is the procedure that such an application will probably entail.

Assessment of applications
Any application that you make to a subsidy body will probably be assessed by a specialist committee: in practice, very small amounts are sometimes allocated on 'officer's discretion' within certain policy lines, but these are very small amounts and it is not usual. The committee system may seem very impersonal but impersonality is assumed to preclude bribery and corruption.

These committee members decide on what and on whom the money available is spent. They are prepared and briefed by the visual arts officer and they may or may not do as that officer recommends, so if you ever have a visit from one of these officers, they can only suggest what they think a committee decision will be and not prejudge it. This may seem a complicated way of doing things but it is the democratic way and democracy 'might not be much good but it's the best thing we've come up with'.

Suppose that you have presented your application, then what happens? Sometimes there will be a studio visit, sometimes work is requested, sometimes there is a shortlist and interviews held and sometimes not. The agreed criteria for grant aid is 'quality of work' and then three difficulties arise; first, to recognise quality and agree on it; second, practical considerations always present themselves; and finally, the amount of money available is always several times insufficient for the demands made upon it. But the following considerations are endemic and perhaps few applicants realise how seriously they are discussed.

- *Is your work good enough?* It is difficult to be objective about this, but 'good of its sort' is a measure.
- *Does your application fit with existing policies?* If it has been decided to give no travel grants, your request to go and photograph wind damage on Turkish minarets will fail. An alert officer will direct you to travel scholarships.
- *Does your work duplicate other work currently being grant aided?* If you are the fourth landscape painter or raku potter to be seen that day, you may be rejected on these grounds.
- *Do you appear to be serious in your work and likely to develop?*
- *Would you use the money well and do you need it?* While no obvious means test is operated, some consideration is usually given to this.

Luck also plays a part in these decisions. Because there is a constant turnover of around a third of committee members, there is no body of case-law and decisions can be inconsistent. There may also be local political considerations; for example, if a remote district has been contributing to the RAA for years and no grants have ever been made within its territory and an artist applies from it, all other things being equal, geography may sway the balance in that applicant's favour.

On a broader political and 'controversial' front, committees can be quite daring because it will rest at the back of their collective mind that the press loves controversy and any publicity is good publicity. But one factor that few would admit is that slightly less able artists *can* tend to get the grants because they are the ones who need help and the abler ones will fight their own corner. Strong work can divide a committee while gentler work will more easily gain a consensus. There is now very considerable effort to benefit minority groups and the disabled, and to redress the balance of grant giving in their favour.

Being turned down for a grant can seem like a public condemnation of your work and it is a result that is very difficult to query. There is no court of appeal and letters to directors only make you unpopular. When the disappointment has worn off, you could ask the visual arts officer's opinion whether you should apply again and if they are good natured and you do not show that you are aggrieved, they may discuss it. But it is to combat this disappointment that the criteria for decision making has been described so fully.

Other schemes and network benefits
Refer back to the list of schemes that the RAAs run and you will see that grants are only one of them. The residencies, payments, art for public places, and studio grants all carry their own descriptions and conditions and dates of application.

Money is one benefit that the RAAs can offer to clients and the other is that between them they can sometimes offer publicity and exposure of your work. Since there is a network of contact in any profession, once you are on it you can become known to that profession more quickly than otherwise. All the RAAs run an index of artists in their region and some are published, some not.

Apart from the indexes run by the RAAs and the Crafts Council, there are others set up by independent agencies, usually for some specific purpose or part of the country. Your RAA should direct you to them or you could read about them in *Artists Newsletter* or *artyfacts*.

Perhaps this is the place to mention some recently established specific provision for the recognition and presentation of women's work, unnecessary in an ideal world but still required in our imperfect situation. The Women Artists Slide Library collects information on women artists, past and present, from all over the world. It is a reference library which holds a mass of data on contemporary women artists, on those who are dead but whose work is catalogued and on the documentation of exhibitions and events that include women artists. This enterprising scheme is expanding to include taped conversations and videos of women artists and its journal and publications are well worth pursuing.

These indexes and the national bodies rely to an extent on the officers of the RAAs to talent spot for them. Although there are few officers in this countrywide system they tend to be in personal contact with one another. Accusations that this is really another branch of the Mafia are not appropriate because, while they may all know one another, they certainly do not agree and united action between such independent bodies does not often happen.

This network was set up with the highest of intentions and on paper it looks foolproof. The effect that it has on the art world is indisputable to those who operate the system but sometimes doubtful to outsiders. Three factors perhaps mar its performance: the regions are underfunded and too large for such small staff to make a significant impact; the RAAs are suspicious of all commercial activity; and finally, they tend to project their image only for the converted and not for outsiders. In one recent set of annual reports, only one described the nature or status of its organisation in such a way that an outsider who had never heard of them could understand it. This introspective approach is unlikely to attract the outside funding of which they are all in need.

Local arts councils and associations

For once the terms 'council' and 'association' are interchangeable and do not imply different sorts of organisation.

The national arts councils have national responsibilities, the RAAs have regional responsibilities, for possibly one but usually four or more counties, and the local arts organisations are usually concerned with one local authority district which may be a single town such as Leicester or Oxford. They are instigated and run by professional and amateur enthusiasts for the arts and often one art form such as drama or crafts will predominate. Sometimes the secretary of such a group is a local authority officer but they are always voluntary and not local authority directed even though their income will be from a local authority grant. This amount can vary from a few hundred pounds to £30,000 but this last figure is very rare and their average income is about £5000 of which some may also come from the RAA.

There are about 120 such organisations and their quality and effectiveness varies a lot. In an area where there are a number of institutes of higher education, the local arts council (or association) will probably consist of people professionally concerned with the arts and their activities will reflect this. But in a rural area or somewhere with little professional employment, the local arts body will probably be amateur dominated and be no less interesting for that because some of them are very ingenious and involve a whole community in activities.

In order to find out whether the area where you live is an area served by such a body, either contact your RAA, or else contact the National Association of Local Arts Councils to which about half of them are affiliated, or ask the local authority. It could be worth your time to do so because although they may have nothing to offer, you could be included in an extensive and nationally advertised 'Open Studio Week' as in Oxford, or get financial help. Your RAA will be most likely to tell you about them and whether they simply run a village bunfight or give grants to professional artists.

The previous advice for applications and description of typical assessment will apply to any application, whether a prestigious Churchill Travel Fellowship or planning permission for a workshop. If you decide to apply to your local arts council or association, find out first how much money they have and the pattern of expenditure. Then apply accordingly. Even a small amount of money at the right moment can make a difference to your career.

Sponsorship and patronage

By grants and benefits the public bodies are able to subsidise the individual artist. Subsidy is normally associated with public money, and sponsorship and patronage with non-government money from business or some other source. Thus, Covent Garden Opera House is subsidised

by the Arts Council but sponsored by Sainsburys. In recent years there
has been encouragement by the Arts Council and also promptings by the
deepening economic recession for clients to seek sponsorship as well as
claiming subsidy. Therefore, if you look at a programme from one of the
large London Theatres or one of the main regional theatres, acknowledgements will be made with tactful, graphic modesty to the subsidising
bodies and probably with rather more flamboyance to the sponsors.

It is very unusual for individuals to receive patronage or sponsorship
but sometimes a gallery pays an artist a stipend against unsold work and
occasionally gives an advance on sales, but to the big names and not the
impecunious hopeful. Information about other instances of patronage is
guarded because these are private transactions. There are also scholarships and bursaries from different sources that are offered usually for very
specific academic, artistic or scientific purposes. They are advertised in
the appropriate periodicals such as *Artists' Newsletter* and in the national
press such as the Monday *Guardian* and you just have to keep looking, but
here some advice given in other chapters holds good; look slightly outside
your profession and use opportunities of a more general nature. For
example, the Churchill Travelling Fellowships are advertised in the
local RDC newsletter alongside the sale of pug-mills and transformers.
The charities set up to promote a particular purpose or group of people
do not advertise in the same way but can sit quietly and accumulate
interest on unclaimed funds. They are listed in various publications of
which the complete (or virtually complete) list is in the *Directory of Grant
Giving Trusts* but in order not to be overwhelmed by the number of trusts,
you could read it in conjunction with the *Guide to Major Grant Making
Trusts* published by the Directory of Social Change, and which makes
some sense of the jungle.

The difference between sponsorship and patronage is that sponsorship
suggests that something is expected in return like advertisement of a
name on a box at the opera or in the title, and patronage does not carry
an expectation of direct return but offers benefits simply on the value of
the exercise. One of the best known examples of sponsorship for the
visual arts was the John Moores Liverpool Exhibition which was run
biennially from 1957 to 1987.

Appendices

Appendix 1

Useful Addresses

This list includes some addresses that are not normally associated with the art world and omits a number that are. It includes all those that have been mentioned in the text but a brief description of purpose is given where it is not self-evident for those organisations which have not previously been described. For comprehensive address and book lists the reader should consult the following publications:

Directory of Exhibition Spaces: Artic Producers Ltd
The Artists Directory: Art Guide Publications
Running a Workshop: Crafts Council

General addresses

ACME House Association
15 Robinson Road, London E2 9LX; 01-981 6811

Artists' Agency
17 Grange Terrace, Stockton Road, Sunderland SR2 7DF; 091 5109318.
The agency operates in Northern Arts region and provides residencies in a variety of settings for artists, photographers, craftspeople, writers and practitioners in any art form.

Artist's Cards
Abacus (Colour Printers) Ltd, Lowick, Near Ulverston, Cumbria LA12 8DX; 0229 85 361

Arts for Health
Faculty of Art and Design, Department of Architecture and Landscape, Loxford Tower, Lower Chatham Street, Manchester M15 6HA; 061-236 8916

Association for Business Sponsorship of the Arts
2 Chester Street, London SW1X 7BB; 01-235 9781. ABSA encourages the growth of sponsorship by business organisations of the arts in this country.

British Broadcasting Corporation
Broadcasting House, London W1A 1AA; 01-580 4468

The Building Centre
26 Store Street, London WC1E 7BT; 01-637 1022

Common Ground (New Milestones Project)
45 Shelton Street, Covent Garden, London WC2H 9HJ; 01-379 3109

Co-operative Development Agency
Broadmead House, 21 Panton Street, London SW1Y 4DR; 01-839 2988

Equal Opportunities Commission
Overseas House, Quay Street, Manchester M3 3HN; 061-833 9244
London office:
1 Bedford Street, London WC2E 9HD; 01-379 6323

Gulbenkian Foundation (UK Branch)
98 Portland Place, London W1N 4ET; 01-636 5313. The work of the
Gulbenkian Foundation in the UK is organised around programmes in
arts, education and social welfare. Grants are made to individuals for
projects that are in accordance with policy; and some Foundation
projects invite application and these are advertised in the art press.

Independent Broadcasting Authority
70 Brompton Road, London SW3 1EY; 01-584 7011

Interchange Trust (formerly Interaction Centre)
15 Wilkin Street, London NW5 3NG; 01-267 9421. Interchange is a
development agency and resource centre from which a programme of
community arts and education projects is run.

Law Centres Federation
Duchess House, 18-19 Warren Street, London W1P 5DP; 01-387 8570

The Law Society
113 Chancery Lane, London WC2A 1PL; 01-242 1222

Legal Aid Head Office
Newspaper House,
8-16 Great New Street, London EC4A 3BN; 01-353 7411

The Loft Shop
Progress Way, Croydon, Surrey CR0 4XD; 01-681 4060

The National Art Education Archive
Bretton Hall College, West Bretton, Wakefield, West Yorkshire WF4 4LG; 092 465 261

National Campaign for the Arts
Francis House, Francis Street, London SW1P 1DE; 01-828 4448. This was created in 1984 by artists, administrators, employers' organisations and trade unions to create a united campaign for the performing, composing, visual, community and ethnic arts.

Public Art Development Trust
6-8 Rosebery Avenue, London EC1R 4TD; 01-837 6070. This organisation was established to encourage and organise commissions for works of art in public spaces.

Royal Institute of British Architects
Clients Advisory Service, 66 Portland Place, London W1N 4AD; 01-580 5588

Rural Crafts Association
Heights Cottage, Brook Road, Wormley, Surrey GU8 5UA; 042 879 2292

Shape London
1 Thorpe Close, London W10 5SL; 01-960 9245. Shape is an arts organisation established in London in 1976 to create opportunities for those who are mentally or physically disabled to participate in arts activities. There are over a dozen other Shape organisations that share similar aims and which can be contacted through the regional arts association.
The nearest Scottish equivalent is Artlink for Edinburgh and the Lothians:

Artlink
4 Forth Street, Edinburgh EH1 3LD; 031-556 6350

SPACE Studios
6-8 Rosebery Avenue, London EC1R 4TD; 01-278 7795

Women Artists Slide Library
Fulham Palace, Bishop's Avenue, London SW6 6EA; 01-731 7618

Arts councils, arts associations and related bodies

National bodies
Arts Council of Great Britain
105 Piccadilly, London W1V 0AU; 01-629 9495

Arts Council of Northern Ireland
181a Stranmillis Road, Belfast BT9 5DJ; 0232 663591

The British Council
10 Spring Gardens, London SW1A 2BN; 01-930 8466

Crafts Council Gallery and Information Centre
12 Waterloo Place, London SW1Y 4AU; 01-930 4811. The administrative offices are at:
1 Oxendon Street, London SW1Y 4AT; same phone number.

The Design Council
28 Haymarket, London SW1Y 4SU; 01-839 8000

Scottish Arts Council
19 Charlotte Square, Edinburgh EH2 4DF; 031-226 6051

Welsh Arts Council
9 Museum Place, Cardiff CS1 3NX; 0222 394711

Regional Arts Associations: (RAAs)
Council of Regional Arts Associations (CORAA)
Litton Lodge, 13A Clifton Road, Winchester, Hampshire SO22 5BP; 0962 51063. This is the secretariat for the RAAs and exists for the co-ordination of their work and to promote their interests at a national level.

Buckinghamshire Arts Association
55 High Street, Aylesbury, Bucks HP20 1SA; 0296 434704. (Buckinghamshire). Founded 1984. The area was omitted during the formation of Southern Arts, Eastern Arts and East Midlands Arts associations, hence the need for its own.

Eastern Arts
Cherry Hinton Hall, Cherry Hinton Road, Cambridge CB1 4DW; 0223

215355. (Bedfordshire, Cambridgeshire, Essex, Hertfordshire, Norfolk, Suffolk).

East Midlands Arts   Nick Scates (vis. Arts)
Mountfields House, Forest Road, Loughborough, Leicestershire LE11 3HU. 0509 218292. (Derbyshire (excluding High Peak district), Leicestershire, Northamptonshire, Nottinghamshire).

Greater London Arts
9 White Lion Street, London N1 9PD; 01-837 8808. (The area of the 32 London boroughs and the City of London). Each London borough also has its own arts staff.

Lincolnshire and Humberside Arts
St Hugh's, Newport, Lincoln LN1 3DN; 0522 33555. (Lincolnshire, Humberside). A mainly rural area.

Merseyside Arts
Bluecoat Chambers, School Lane, Liverpool L1 3BX; 051-709 0671. (Metropolitan County of Merseyside, district of West Lancashire, Ellesmere Port and Halton districts of Cheshire). Covers a small area only.

Northern Arts
10 Osborne Terrace, Jesmond, Newcastle upon Tyne NE2 1NZ; 091-281 6334. (Cleveland, Cumbria, Durham, Northumberland, Metropolitan County of Tyne and Wear). Founded 1961, covers tourist and industrial areas.

North West Arts
12 Harter Street, Manchester M1 6HY; 061-228 3062. (Greater Manchester, High Peak district of Derbyshire, Lancashire (except district of West Lancashire), Cheshire (except Ellesmere Port and Halton districts).

South East Arts
10 Mount Ephraim, Tunbridge Wells, Kent TN4 8AS; 0892 515210. (Kent, Surrey, East Sussex).

Southern Arts
19 Southgate Street, Winchester, Hampshire SO23 9DQ; 0962 55099. (Berkshire, Hampshire, Isle of Wight, Oxfordshire, West Sussex, Wiltshire, districts of Bournemouth, Christchurch and Poole).

South West Arts
Bradninch Place, Gandy Street, Exeter EX4 3LS; 0392 218188. (Avon, Cornwall, Devon, Dorset (except districts of Bournemouth, Christchurch and Poole), Gloucestershire, Somerset).

West Midlands Arts
82 Granville Street, Birmingham B1 2LH; 021-631 3121. (County of Hereford and Worcester, Metropolitan county of West Midlands, Shropshire, Staffordshire, Warwickshire). The highest concentration of population except for the area covered by the Greater London Arts Association.

Yorkshire Arts Association
Glyde House, Glydegate, Bradford, Yorkshire BD5 0BQ; 0274 723051. (North Yorkshire, South Yorkshire, West Yorkshire).

Government departments and agencies

British Overseas Trade Board Offices
1 Victoria Street, London SW1H 0ET; 01-215 7877. Regional offices are in the telephone directory.

Department of Employment
Small Firms Centres. Freefone service; dial 100 and ask for freefone Enterprise: they will tell you your nearest *Small Firms Centre* which offers free services.

Department of Health and Social Security has, from July 1988, been separated into two departments, each with its own Secretary of State. The defunct DHSS will be listed in telephone books for some time, but while their information central offices share an address, they have separate telephone numbers.
Department of Social Security and Department of Health
Information Division, Richmond House, 79 Whitehall, London SW1A 2NS; public enquiries for the Department of Social Security are referred to the Freeline 0800 66555.
DHSS Leaflets (the name is retained for the present)
PO Box 24, Stanmore, Middlesex HA7 1AY; 01-952 2311

Design Registry
The Patent Office, State House, 66-71 High Holborn, London WC1R 4TP; 01-831 2525 (leaflets free on application).

Highlands and Islands Development Board
Bridge House, 27 Bank Street, Inverness IV1 1QR; 0463 234171

Local Enterprise Development Unit
LEDU Business Centre, 17-19 Linenhall Street, Belfast BT2 8AB; 0232 242582

London Enterprise Agency (LEntA)
4 Snow Hill, London EC1A 2BS; 01-236 3000

Rural Development Commission (formerly CoSIRA)
141 Castle Street, Salisbury, Wiltshire SP1 3TP; 0722 336255

Scottish Development Agency
Rosebery House, Haymarket Terrace, Edinburgh EH12 5EZ; 031-337 9595

Training Agency (formerly Manpower Services Commission)
Head Office, Moorfoot, Sheffield S1 4PQ; Information 0742 704318

Welsh Development Agency Headquarters, Pearl House, Grayfriars Road, Cardiff CF1 3XX; 0222 222666

National unions, associations, guilds and similar organisations

The Association of Illustrators
1 Colville Place, London W1P 1HN; 01-636 4100

British and American Arts Association (BAA)
49 Wellington Street, London WC2E 7BN; 01-379 7755. An information and counselling service for artists wishing to cross the Atlantic either way.

British Insurance Brokers' Association
Biba House, 14 Bevis Marks, London EC3N 7AT; 01-623 9043

Chartered Society of Designers
29 Bedford Square, London WC1B 3EG; 01-631 1510

Contemporary Applied Arts
43 Earlham Street, Covent Garden, London WC2H 9LD; 01-836 6993

Contemporary Art Society

Tate Gallery, 20 John Islip Street, London SW1P 4LL; 01-821 5323. The Society was founded in 1910 to promote the development of contemporary art and to acquire work by living artists for gift or loan to public collections.

Craftsmen Potters Association of Great Britain Ltd

21 Carnaby Street, London W1V 1PH; 01-437 6781

Design and Artists Copyright Society Ltd (DACS)

St Mary's Clergy House, 2 Whitechurch Land, London E1 7QR; 01-247 1650

National Artists Association

Co-ordinator, Roland Miller, 49 Stainton Road, Sheffield S11 7AX; 0742 669889

National Association of Arts Centres

Room 110, The Arts Centre, Vane Terrace, Darlington, County Durham DL3 7AX; 0325 465930

National Association of Local Arts Councils

101 Walcot Avenue, Luton, Beds LU2 0PP; 0582 30775

The National Federation of Self-Employed and Small Businesses Ltd

Yorkshire Bank Chambers, 32 St Annes Road West, Lytham St Annes, Lancashire SY8 1NY; 0253 720911
London office: 140 Lower Marsh, London SE1 7AE; 01-928 9272

National Society for Education in Art and Design

7a High Street, Corsham, Wiltshire SN13 0ES; 0249 714825

Printmakers Council

Clerkenwell Workshop, 31 Clerkenwell Close, London EC1R 0AT; 01-250 1927

Further Reading

General and specific interest

Art, Design and Craft – A Manual for Business Success John Crowe, Edward Arnold. £5.95

The Art of Survival Antony Parkin, Antony Parkin Publications 1985; 47 Oxenhill Road, Kemsing, Sevenoaks, Kent TN15 6RG. £3.00

Art Within Reach edited by Peter Townsend, *Art Monthly*, Arts Council and Crafts Council 1984. (This is now out of print but a reference copy is available at the Arts Council library.)

Artists and People Su Braden, Routledge and Kegan Paul 1978.

The Artists Directory Richard Leyzell and Heather Waddell, Art Guide Publications, 3rd edn 1988. £8.95

Arts Address Book Peter Marcan, Peter Marcan Publications 1986; 31 Rowcliff Road, High Wycombe, Buckinghamshire. £4.90

Arts and Disabled People. A report published for Carnegie Trust by Bedford Square Press. £4.95

The Arts Review Year Book Arts Review annual publication; who's who and what's what in the art world. £10.95

Careers in Art and Design Linda Ball, 5th edn, Kogan Page 1989. £3.95

Caution: A guide to safe practice in the arts and crafts Tim Challis and Gary Roberts, Sunderland Polytechnic 1984. £3.50

The Craftsman's Directory Stephen and Jean Lance Publications (annual publication), Brook House, Mint Street, Godalming, Surrey GU7 1HE. £5.00

Directory of Exhibition Spaces edited by Neil Hanson and Susan Jones, Artic Producers, 2nd edn 1988. £9.50

Directory of Grant Making Trusts The Charities Aid Foundation (published in March in alternate years). £45.00

The Economic Situation of the Visual Artist Andrew Brighton and Nicholas Pearson, Gulbenkian Foundation 1985. This is not published but is available in a photocopied edition from the Gulbenkian Foundation for £15. It is also available at selected libraries of which a list can be obtained from the Foundation.

Get it on Radio and Television Jane Drinkwater, Pluto Press; a guide for those wishing to use the media. £3.95

Help! I need somebody Sally Knight, Kimpton; a guide to national associations for people in need. £2.00

London Art and Artists Guide Heather Waddell, Art Guide Publications 1985 5th edn 1988. £5.95

A full list of Art Guide Publications is available from A C Black, 35 Bedford Row, London WC1R 4JH; 01-242 0946.

Making Ways; the visual artists' guide to surviving and thriving edited by David Butler, Artic Producers. £7.95

New Milestones: Sculpture, Community and the Land Joanna Morland for Common Ground 1988. £4.95

Organising Your Own Exhibition Debbie Duffin, ACME. £3.00

The Penguin Guide to the Law John Pritchard. £9.95

Print: how you can do it yourself Jonathan Zeitlyn, Interchange 1985; a guide to doing your own printing and dealing with printers. £3.75

The Professional Practice of Design Dorothy Goslett, Batsford 1980. £9.95

Running a Workshop, Crafts Council 1985; basic business for craftspeople. £3.95

Starting a Business on a Shoestring Michel Syrett and Chris Dunn, Penguin 'Self-starter' series. £3.95

The Visual Artists' Copyright Handbook Henry Lydiate, Artlaw Services Ltd 1983; (available from Design and Artists Copyright Society). £4.35

Wanted: Community Artists Rod Brooks, Gulbenkian Foundation 1988. £2.50

Willing's Press Guide Thomas Skinner Directories (annual publication), Windsor Court, East Grinstead House, East Grinstead, West Sussex RH19 1XE. £49.00

Work for Yourself Chris Parsons and Angela Neustatter, Pan 1980.

Working in Crafts; an independent socio-economic study of craftsmen and women in England and Wales Alex Bruce and Paul Filmer, Crafts Council 1983. (This is now out of print but a reference copy is available at the Crafts Council Information Centre.)

Writers' and Artists' Year Book Adam and Charles Black (annual publication). £5.95

The Directory of Social Change, Radius Works, Back Lane, London NW1 1HL; 01-435 8171. This is an educational charity which, by its publications and seminars, provides information on financial matters (fundraising, accounting, investment etc) mainly to the voluntary sector (that is, to those connected with charities). Their excellent book list, from which a few are listed here, will be most use to those involved in group projects but some for individual needs are also on offer.

National and local government departments and agencies' publications

Department of Employment. Small Firms Service. Dial 100 and ask for freefone Enterprise. Several leaflets are produced of which the most relevant are: *Starting your own business* and the sequel *Running your own business, Accounting for small firms, Employing People, How to start exporting*.

Directory of Postgraduate and Post-experience courses. Council for National Academic Awards, 344-345, Gray's Inn Road, London WC1X 9BP.

A Guide to the Major Grant-Making Trusts 1988-89 edn £12.50. This publication describes 250 of the wealthiest grant-making trusts and is an indispensable guide for those wanting to know whatever there is to know about these sometimes secretive charities.

A Guide to Company Giving 1986-87 edn £12.50. This publication lists the 1,000 UK top companies and gives information about their donations policies.

A Guide to Grants for Individuals in Need 1987-88 edn. £12.50. Most of these charities are to help those in distress from sickness or poverty but there are some that are educational and a few that are specifically for women.

The Educational Grants Directory £12.50. This is for schoolchildren and students but is included as it may help those who seek higher education later in life.

The Arts Funding Guide 1988 £7.95. This new publication is aimed at those running arts organisations or involved in arts projects and who need to raise money.

Raising Money from Government £4.50. How to apply for money from central and local government and from the many government bodies such as the Training Commission.

Raising Money for Women £5.95. The special problems that women encounter in raising money are discussed in this publication.

Should I be Registered for VAT? HM Customs and Excise: local telephone book.

Small Claims in the County Court: How to sue and defend actions without a solicitor. Available free from any County Court: local telephone book.

Starting in Business IR 28. The Board of Inland Revenue: local telephone book.

Art, craft and design periodicals

There are a considerable number of national and international art, craft and design periodicals and the best way to survey them is either in a library at one of the institutes of higher education or at a specialist bookshop such as those run by the Design Centre or the Institute of

Contemporary Art (ICA) in the Mall or, outside London, one of those run by the major arts centres.

Artists Newsletter, PO Box 23, Old Simpson Street School, Simpson Street, Sunderland SR4 6DG

Art Monthly, 36 Great Russell Street, London WC1B 3PP

Artscribe, 39 North Road, London N7 9DP

Arts Review, 16 St James Gardens, London W11 4RE

Artyfacts, published by the Careers Unit, Brighton Polytechnic, Grand Parade, Brighton BN2 2JY; 0273 604141 ext. 272

Ceramic Review, 21 Carnaby Street, London W1V 1PH

Combined Arts, 7 Anglo Terrace, Bath BA1 5HN; 0225 337895

Combined Arts Bulletin is free on request and *Craft History, the International Quarterly of Mediaeval and Modern Craftsmanship* is £36 an annual subscription and £13.95 per issue.

Crafts, Crafts Council, 1 Oxendon Street, London SW1Y 4AT

Designer, Chartered Society of designers, 29 Bedford Square, London WC1B 3EG

Modern Painters, 10 Barley Mow Passage, London W4 4PH

Books from Kogan Page

Debt Collection Made Easy, Peter Buckland

How to Choose Business Premises: A Guide for the Small Firm, Howard Green, Brian Chalkley and Paul Foley

Starting a Successful Small Business, 2nd edn, M J Morris

The Stoy Hayward Business Tax Guide 1988-89, Mavis Seymour and Stephen Say

Successful Marketing for the Small Business, 2nd edn, Dave Patten

Working for Yourself: The Daily Telegraph Guide to Self-Employment, 10th edition, Godfrey Golzen

Writing for a Living, 2nd edn, Ian Linton

Index

Accident and sickness 19
  insurance against 60–61
accountants 36–7
accounts, keeping 29
ACME 66, 70, 73–4, 133
addresses, useful 133–6
administration 40
advisory panels 124
agents 89
alternative skills, using 112–13
archives 50
Arnolfini, Bristol 99
Art for Public Places 125
Art Monthly 46, 88, 91, 145
Art Within Reach 9, 55, 141
Artist's and Craftsman's Tax Handbook,
  The 32
Artists' cards 95–6, 133
Artists Directory, The 66, 141
Artists Newsletter 46, 62, 92, 128, 130,
  144
Artists Studio Handbook 70
Artists Union 61
Arts Council of Great Britain 33, 73,
  78, 97, 99, 115, 116–19, 124, 130,
  136
Arts Council of Northern Ireland 115,
  120, 136
Arts for Health 54, 133
Arts Review 46, 93, 144
Artyfacts 92, 128, 144
Assisted Purchase 118
Association of Illustrators 77, 139

Banks 37, 42–3, 71
Banner Arts 9
Bradford Print Biennale 98
British Broadcasting Corporation
  (BBC) 90–91, 134
British Council, The 115, 122–3, 136
British Crafts Centre, see
  Contemporary Applied Arts

British Film Institute 115
Building Centre 72, 134
building regulations 69, 72, 81, 122
buying property 70–71

Camden Lock Market 14
capital gains tax 34–5, 72
capital items 29–30
care of work 87, 89
cash flow 43
Chartered Society of Designers 61, 139
Churchill Travel Fellowships 130
Citizens Advice Bureau (CAB) 51–2,
  59, 70
City Gallery, Milton Keynes 105
Collected Artlaw Articles 87
Collectorplan 119
Combined Arts 92, 144
Community Programme 48
Community Programme Unit 90
Companies Act 56
Companies Registration Office 58
competitions 108
Contemporary Applied Arts 61, 139
Contemporary Art Society 107, 140
contracts 52–3
  of commission 53–5, 81
  of employment 60
  for an exhibition 101–2
  with a gallery 100–101
  with a printer 94–5
  of sale 87–8
contributory benefits 17–18, 21
Co-operative Development Agency 57,
  134
copyright 54, 75–9, 87, 102
correspondence, *see* letters
Council for Small Industries in Rural
  Areas, *see* Rural Development
  Commission
county courts 44–5, 123
Covent Garden markets 83

craft fairs 106-7
Crafts 121, 144
Crafts Council 33, 66, 70, 74, 90,99,
103, 107, 116, 120-22, 136
Craftsman's Directory, The 106, 141
creditors 45, 109
curriculum vitae 40, 100
Customs and Excise, Board of 26, 90,
143

Debtors 43-5, 109-10
deductible expenses 28-9, 76
Department of Employment 49, 143
Department of Health and Social
Security (DHSS) 11, 16-25, 56,
59, 138
Design and Artists Copyright Society
(DACS) 78-9, 84, 140
design and technology 45-6
Design Council, The 115, 122, 136
Design Enterprise Fund 49
Design Registry 79-80
development corporations 123
Directory of Exhibition Spaces 98, 103,
141
Directory of Grant Giving Trusts 130, 141
Directory of Social Change 130, 142
East Midlands Arts 137
Eastern Arts 108, 136
*Economic Situation of the Visual Artist,
The* 10, 119, 141
Education, Department of 11
Embroiderers Guild 107
employing staff 47, 59-60
Employment, Department of 47, 49,
103
enterprise agencies 48
Enterprise Allowance Scheme 48
Equal Opportunities Commission
55-6, 134
Equal Pay Act 32
estate agents 66
estimates 94
exhibitions 99-102; *and see* galleries

Fairs 106-7
family credit 19
festivals 106-7
Fibre Art 107
filing 41

Galleries 14, 89-90, 97-102
Graduate Enterprise Programme 49
grants 33-4, 113, 115-16, 125-7
graphic design and layout 95
group shows 105
*Guide to Safe Practice in the Arts and
Crafts A*, 81-2
Gulbenkian Foundation 78, 83, 134

Hayward Gallery 117
Health Service 54
holograms 83
home improvement grants 73
hospitals 105
housing aid 51
Hyde Park railings displays 14, 107

Improvement grants 73
income 11-15
income support 19-22, 109, 112, 113
income tax 12, 15, 26-34, 56, 57, 59,
65-6, 112
Independent Broadcasting Authority
(IBA) 91, 134
Inland Revenue, Board of 20, 26-7,
31-4, 143
insurance 60-61, 82
insurance brokers 81, 139
International Contemporary Art Fair
107
ITV, *see* Independent Broadcasting
Authority

Jobcentres 47, 59
John Moores Liverpool Exhibition
108, 130
John Player Portrait Awards 14, 108

Land Registry 71
Law Centres 51, 70, 134
Law Society 51, 134
leases 68
Legal Aid Schemes 51
legal matters 50-56
Leicestershire Education Authority
Art Collection 123
letters, writing 40-41, 67-8, 100
Liberty's One Off-Shop 103
libraries 105, 123
licence to occupy premises 68-9
limited companies 31, 58

Liverpool Garden Festival 123
Loan Guarantee Scheme 42
loans 12, 16, 41–2, 113
local arts councils/associations 66, 107, 115, 128–9
local authorities 15, 28, 43, 64, 66–9, 81, 87, 97–8, 99, 104, 106–7, 108, 122–3
local press 93
local radio stations 92, 107
location 63–4
Loft Shop, the 71, 135
London Ecology Centre 108
London Enterprise Agency (LEntA) 48

Magazines 92, 103, 111
making a loss 30–32
Manpower Services Commission, *see* Training Agency
market place 97–109
market trends 82–3
marketing 85–95
maternity leave 112–13
means tested benefits 17, 19
Merseyside Development Corporation 123
Milton Keynes Development Corporation 123
mortgages 64, 70
Municipal Year Book 123
Museums Association Yearbook 98

National Artists Association 61–2, 140
National Association of Local Arts Councils 129, 140
National Federation of Self-Employed and Small Businesses 61
National Insurance contributions 12, 15, 17, 21, 22–5, 47, 56, 59–60, 112
National Society for Education in Art and Design (NSEAD) 61, 140
newspapers 66, 91–2, 106, 110, 111
non-contributory benefits 17, 19
Northern Arts 124, 137

open studio 103
Open Studio Week, Oxford 129
Oriel 119
outdoor sites 107

overdraft 42–3
Oxfordshire Visual Arts Festival 107

Parish councils 123
part-time work 112–13
partnerships 31, 56–7
Patent Office 79, 80
patents 80
patronage 129–30
Pay As You Earn (PAYE) 12, 27–8, 47, 59, 112; *and see* income tax
Payment for Exhibiting 102, 118
pensions 12, 15, 18
Performing Rights Society 89
periodicals 93
personal allowance 33
planning regulations 65–6, 70, 73, 81, 104, 110, 116, 122
premises 63–74
press release 91–2
pricing of artefacts 13
pricing your time 14–15
printers 94–5
Printmakers Council 61, 140
product, your 75–84, 86
product liability 80–81
Professional and Executive Recruitment (PER) 47–8
Professional and Executive Register 47–8
Protection of Industrial Designs 79–80
Public Lending Right 89
publicity 90–94

Quotations 94

Race Relations Act 59
radio and television 90–91
reception 39–40
regional arts associations (RAAs) 33, 37, 53, 54, 66, 70, 74, 78, 89, 92, 99, 102, 103, 105, 106–7, 115–20, 123–9
registered designs 79–80
Resale Royalties 88–9
residencies 28, 43, 118, 125
Royal Academy 107
Royal Institute of British Architects (RIBA) 72, 135
Royal Over-Seas League 107
royalties on resale 88–9

Rufford Crafts Centre 123
Running a Workshop 43, 61, 90, 142
Rural Crafts Association 107
Rural Development Area grants 63, 73
Rural Development Commission 37,
    49–50, 72–4, 103, 107, 130, 139

Safety in manufacturing processes
    81–2
Sale of Goods Act 52
sale or return 100
selling 87–9, 97–108
selling abroad 90
Serpentine Gallery 117
Sex Discrimination Act 32, 55–6, 59
Scottish Arts Council 115, 119–20, 136
Scottish Development Agency 107,
    120, 139
shops 103
small claims procedure 44–5
Small Firms Centres 49, 138
social security, *see* Department of
    Health and Social Security
Society of Industrial Artists and
    Designers, *see* Chartered Society
    of Designers
sole trader 31, 56
SPACE 66, 70, 73–4, 135
specialist press 92–3, 111–12
sponsorship 113, 129–30
stipend agreement 101, 130
studios 28, 40, 63
    open 103–4
    running costs 69–70
subsidy 113, 115–20
supplementary benefit, *see* income
    support

Tate Gallery 108
tax schedules 27–32, 65
teaching 11–12, 28, 112
technical development 83–4
temporary work 112
tenant's costs 69–70
Tolly Cobbold Eastern Arts National
    Exhibition 108
touring work 102–3
town councils 123
Trade and Industry, Department of
    46, 103
trade marks 80
trade unions 60–61
Training Agency (formerly the MSC)
    47–8, 53, 139
Turner Prize 108

Unemployment benefit 18, 109
unincorporated associations 57–8

Value added tax (VAT) 14, 26, 35–6,
    46, 56, 94
Visual Artists' Copyright Handbook, The
    78, 142

Walker Art Gallery 108
Welsh Arts Council 115, 119–20, 136
Welsh Crafts Council 107
West Midlands Arts 126, 138
Whitworth Museum 98
Willing's Press Guide 90, 142
word processors 38, 40
working at home 64–5
Working in Crafts 10, 121, 142
Working to Commission 55
Writers' and Artists' Year Book 111, 142